The Electoral Origins
of Divided Government

TRANSFORMING AMERICAN POLITICS
Lawrence C. Dodd, Series Editor

Dramatic changes in political institutions and behavior over the past two decades have underscored the dynamic nature of American politics, confronting political scientists with a new and pressing intellectual agenda. The pioneering work of early postwar scholars, while laying a firm empirical foundation for contemporary scholarship, failed to consider how American politics might change or to recognize the forces that would make fundamental change inevitable. In reassessing the static interpretations fostered by these classic studies, political scientists are now examining the underlying dynamics that generate transformational change.

Transforming American Politics will bring together texts and monographs that address four closely related aspects of change. A first concern is documenting and explaining recent changes in American politics—in institutions, processes, behavior, and policymaking. A second is reinterpreting classic studies and theories to provide a more accurate perspective on postwar politics. The series will look at historical change to identify recurring patterns of political transformation within and across the distinctive eras of American politics. Last and perhaps most importantly, the series will present new theories and interpretations that explain the dynamic processes at work and thus clarify the direction of contemporary politics. All of the books will focus on the central theme of transformation—transformation in both the conduct of American politics and in the way we study and understand its many aspects.

TITLES IN THIS SERIES

The Electoral Origins of Divided Government

COMPETITION IN
U.S. HOUSE ELECTIONS, 1946–1988

Gary C. Jacobson
University of California–San Diego

Westview Press
BOULDER • SAN FRANCISCO • OXFORD

Transforming American Politics

Copyright © 1990 by Westview Press, Inc.

Published in 1990 in the United States of America by Westview Press, Inc., 5500 Central Avenue, Boulder, Colorado 80301, and in the United Kingdom by Westview Press, Inc., 36 Lonsdale Road, Summertown, Oxford OX2 7EW

Library of Congress Cataloging-in-Publication Data
Jacobson, Gary C.
  The electoral origins of divided government : competition in U.S. House elections, 1946–1988 / Gary C. Jacobson.
    p. cm. — (Transforming American politics series)
  Includes bibliographical references and index.
  ISBN 0-8133-0906-9 (hardcover) — ISBN 0-8133-0907-7 (pbk.)
  1. United States. Congress. House—Elections. 2. Elections— United States. 3. United States—Politics and government—1945–   .
I. Title. II. Series.
JK1965.J33 1990
324.973'092—dc20
                                                                                90-12411
                                                                                CIP

Printed and bound in the United States of America

The paper used in this publication meets the requirements of the American National Standard for Permanence of Paper for Printed Library Materials Z39.48-1984.

10   9   8   7   6   5   4   3   2   1

To Winnifred Finch Brown
1883–1976

Contents

Tables and Figures

TABLES

FIGURES

Preface

My initial purpose in writing this book was to examine and explain the evolution of competition in postwar elections to the U.S. House of Representatives. As the work progressed, what I had expected to be a subsidiary issue, the electoral origins of divided party control of the federal government, emerged as the thematic core. The 1988 elections posed the question in starkest terms: How did the Democrats maintain—indeed, increase—their solid House majority despite yet another comfortable victory for the Republican presidential candidate? More generally, Why do Americans now habitually elect Republican presidents and Democratic congresses?

Explanations for the Democrats' continued dominance of Congress fall into two basic categories: structural and political. My analysis ultimately leads me to conclude that all of the structural explanations are either wrong or inadequate and that all of the political explanations are at least partially right. Divided party control reflects, rather than thwarts, popular preferences and so is likely to continue.

The evidence I offer for these views comes from a variety of sources. Like virtually everyone who studies Congress, I made extensive use of data initially gathered and published by the people at Congressional Quarterly, Inc. (CQ). CQ's *Guide to U.S. Elections* was my principal source for electoral data, and the *Congressional Quarterly Weekly Report* was the source for a great deal more, including much of my information about congressional candidates and some district-level presidential election results. I also extensively used CQ's biennial *Politics in America* and Michael Barone and Grant Ujifusa's biennial *Almanac of American Politics*. It is difficult to overstate the value of these sources to students of congressional elections and politics.

I am grateful to Adam Clymer of the *New York Times*, who put me on the distribution list for the *New York Times*/CBS News Poll. I found these polls extraordinarily useful for exploring the political roots of divided government, and they form the heart of Chapter 6. I also made use of data from the 1986 American National Election Study, which was supplied by the Inter-University Consortium for Political and Social

Research. The data were originally collected by the Center for Political Studies of the Institute for Social Research at the University of Michigan, under a grant from the National Science Foundation. Of course, neither the original collectors of the data nor the consortium bear any responsibility for my analyses and interpretations.

Other data sources are cited in due course. I collected some of the original data with the support of a grant from the National Science Foundation (SES-80-77) and, later, with research funds provided by the University of California–San Diego (UCSD).

I performed all of the data analyses with Jeffrey Dubin and Douglas Rivers's Statistical Software Tools (SST), which I found ideally fast and flexible for my purposes. Only scholars who remember the days of punched cards and counter-sorters can fully appreciate the contribution that modern software and hardware make to empirical analysis. I am obliged to Douglas Rivers for making sure I always had the latest version of SST to play with.

Because this book grows out of several lines of research that I have conducted over more than a decade, it is impossible to acknowledge everyone who has contributed to it in some way. But I especially thank my colleagues at UCSD—Nathaniel Beck, Amy Bridges, Gary Cox, Samuel Kernell, Mathew McCubbins, and Samuel Popkin—for sharing their knowledge, insights, and, in Amy Bridges's case, editorial skills. I also thank Douglas Rivers and Gary King for uncovering some errors in the data, Morris Fiorina for helpful comments and suggestions, Donald Green and Michael MacKuen for sharing unpublished results, and Markus Crepaz for his research assistance.

Gary C. Jacobson

1

Introduction

The 1988 House elections produced the smallest turnover in American electoral history. A mere 9 seats switched party control, the fewest ever; 402 of the 408 incumbents seeking reelection were returned to office. Only 7.6% of representatives elected to the 101st Congress were newcomers, the lowest proportion on record.

The chief beneficiaries of stasis were the House Democrats. Despite George Bush's comfortable victory over the Democratic presidential candidate, Michael Dukakis, the Democrats lost only 3 House seats while taking 6 from the Republicans to reach a 260–175 majority.

The election left House Republicans frustrated and angry. Their party has won five of the last six presidential elections, twice by landslides. It controlled the Senate for most of the 1980s and has a reasonable hope of retaking it in the 1990s. Its national campaign committees have outstripped the Democrats' committees in fundraising and organization. The Democrats' lead in party identification, which exceeded twenty points at the time Richard Nixon was first elected president, has been narrowed so far that, in 1988, the parties were in a virtual dead heat among people who reported voting (Wattenberg 1990). Yet Republicans have made no headway in the House, where they have not won a majority since 1952 and have not won more than 192 seats—26 short of a majority—since 1956.

In the aftermath of the 1988 elections, Republican leaders settled on structural explanations for their failure to advance in the House. Democrats continue to win, they argue, because of gerrymandered districts, abuse of the franking privilege and other perquisites of office, and a campaign finance system strongly biased against challengers. With characteristic understatement, Republican Whip Newt Gingrich summed up the charge: "the left-wing in the House is engaged in a conspiracy to avoid fair elections" (Cook 1989:1060).

The Republican view reflects much of the recent scholarly literature on congressional elections. It echoes arguments first offered in the early 1970s, when a similar period of electoral stasis inspired path-breaking work to document and explain an apparent increase in the electoral

1

value of incumbency in House elections. The most important systemic implication of this research was that the enhanced incumbency advantage would insulate the House against changes in national sentiments. With wider margins of safety, House incumbents could ride out contrary electoral trends that in earlier times would have delivered their seats to the other party. The growing incumbency advantage would thus inhibit the translation of vote swings into seat swings in House elections.

Republican leaders claim that this is exactly what has happened; House Democrats have exploited the advantages of incumbency to retain control despite the growing popular preference for Republican candidates and policies. A principal theme of this book is that this view, however comforting to Republicans, is mistaken. Although the advantages conferred by incumbency have grown, this phenomenon falls far short of explaining why the Democrats still dominate the House of Representatives. The House Republicans' fundamental problems are political, not structural.

Furthermore, growth in the electoral value of House incumbency is neither the only nor, arguably, the most important change in competition for House seats during the postwar period. It is part of a more general pattern of change engendered by the loosening of electoral constraints once maintained by party loyalty. Among other things, this development has increased both parties' opportunities to take territory once held exclusively by the opposition. In House elections, Democrats have exploited their expanded opportunities more effectively than have Republicans. How and why they have done so is another focus of this book.

More generally, I examine a variety of changes in competition for House seats in postwar elections with an eye to showing how these changes have contributed to divided party control of the federal government. My assumption is that a more precise view of postwar electoral patterns will lead to a clearer understanding of what has happened. It will also help to set recent electoral trends in wider perspective, providing a counterweight to the pervasive handwringing about the "end of electoral competition" that the 1988 elections seem to have inspired (Rovner 1988).

I begin in the next chapter by documenting the thorough partisan disintegration of electoral politics over the past forty years. Divided control of the federal government is only one manifestation of a more general phenomenon: the progressive dissociation of electoral outcomes across offices with overlapping constituencies and for the same offices across elections. This change reflects a substantial decline in the importance of party cues to voters. The decay of partisanship has made it easier for House incumbents to build personal, rather than impersonally partisan, electoral coalitions and so has enhanced their ability to hold out against contrary partisan tides. But it has also introduced greater electoral volatility and opened the way for parties to win seats that loyally partisan electorates had once denied them.

In Chapter 3 I reexamine changes in the House incumbency advantage over the postwar period. I argue that growth in the incumbency advantage has been, in important respects, overstated and that insufficient attention has been paid to a complementary change: the parties' diminishing ability to retain seats when the incumbent dies or retires. That Republican House candidates have taken no net advantage of expanded competition for open seats argues strongly against the view that Democratic incumbency is responsible for divided government.

Chapter 4 examines changes in opposition to incumbents in House elections. The growth of candidate-centered electoral politics has increased the electoral importance of individual challengers and campaigns. In recent years, the quality of Republican challengers has not varied systematically with the party's national prospects, and in the 1980s, Republicans suffered from a notable dearth of experienced challengers. The aggregate weakness of Republican challengers thus stands as one source of the party's inability to take House seats from Democrats. Both parties have been concentrating campaign money and experienced candidates in fewer contests, especially those for open seats. The dearth of serious competition in the late 1980s derives far more from the weakness of challengers than from an increase in the electoral strength of incumbents.

In the fifth chapter, I search for the structural underpinnings of divided government. I find that none of the common structural explanations for continued Democratic hegemony in the House—including, in addition to the incumbency advantage, a declining swing-ratio, gerrymandering, and campaign finance regulation—withstands serious scrutiny. The roots of divided government are not structural, but political, or so I argue in the sixth, and final, chapter. Republicans have failed to advance in the House because they have fielded inferior candidates on the wrong side of issues that are important to voters in House elections and because voters find it difficult to assign blame or credit when control of government is divided between the parties.

I conclude that the low turnover of House seats in the late 1980s does not mean that the distribution of House seats is insensitive to changes in voters' preferences (or that voters' preferences are immune to national forces), though the connections have become more contingent, depending to a greater extent on candidates and campaigns. Divided government reflects, rather than thwarts, the electorate's will, and it gives rise to a number of self-maintaining forces. Thus we should be prepared to live with divided government as a normal, if not constant, feature of American politics for some time to come.

2

All Politics Is Local: Electoral Disintegration in the Postwar Era

Republicans have won seven of eleven presidential elections since 1948, including five of the last six. Since 1968, Republican presidential candidates have received an average of 55% of the major-party popular vote and a remarkable 78% of the major-party electoral vote. Yet Republicans have not won a majority in the House of Representatives since 1952 and have not won more than 192 House seats—44% of the total—since 1956.

Democratic dominance of the House emerged from the Reagan era fully intact. In elections from 1980 through 1988, with Ronald Reagan at the top of the ticket, in the White House, or both, and despite strong Republican gains in party identification (see Chapter 6), Democrats won an average of 257 House seats (59.0%), slightly greater than their 1946–1978 average of 253 (58.3%). Divided government originates in sharply and consistently divergent election outcomes for the House and the White House.

THE EMERGENCE OF DIVIDED GOVERNMENT

Electoral splits of this sort were once rare. Only once in the twenty-five presidential elections between 1856 and 1952 did the party winning a majority of the popular two-party vote for president fail to organize the House (it happened in 1888). Since 1956, six of the nine presidential elections have delivered split verdicts, all, of course, coinciding with Republican presidential victories. The origin of gap between presidential and House results predates the 1950s, however; it begins with the New Deal realignment. This is clear from Figure 2.1, which displays the partisan distribution of the two-party presidential vote and of House seats from 1876 through 1988.

5

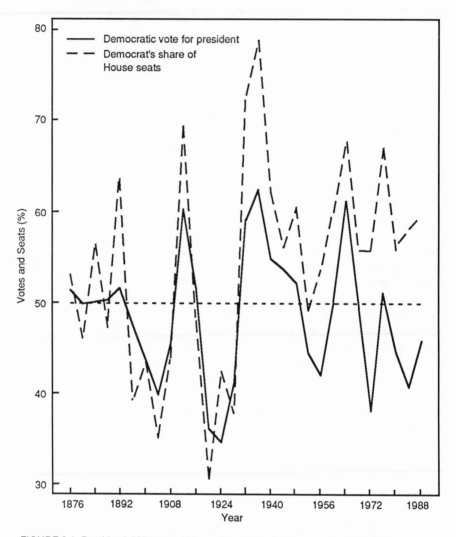

FIGURE 2.1 Presidential Votes and House Seats Won by Democrats, 1876–1988

Prior to 1932, presidential and House results moved together above and below the 50% line, with the House division usually looking like an amplified version of presidential division. The mean difference derived by subtracting the Democrats' share of House seats from presidential votes between 1876 and 1928 was 0.19 percentage points. Since 1932, Democrats have always won a noticeably larger percentage of House seats than of presidential votes. Between 1932 and 1964, the gap averaged 8.9 percentage points; since 1968, it has averaged 13.7 percentage points.

Only once since the New Deal (1952) has a Republican presidential majority coincided with a Republican House majority.

Democratic hegemony in the House has not been confined to presidential elections during the postwar period, of course; Democrats have been equally dominant in midterm elections. Figure 2.2 displays the partisan division of House seats produced by all elections since 1946. Democrats have won an average of 255 House seats in presidential election years, 254 seats at the midterm.

For comparison, Figure 2.2 also displays the partisan distribution of Senate seats. The contrast is striking, though even in Senate elections Republicans have fallen considerably short of the standard set by Republican presidential candidates. Through the early 1970s, the Democrats' share of House and Senate seats tended to coincide, though with an obvious lag because only one-third of Senate seats are at stake in any election year. When Republicans won control of the Senate, they also won control of the House. Since then, however, Republicans have done much better in Senate than in House elections, enjoying majority control after the 1980, 1982, and 1984 elections, while Democratic control of the House was never seriously threatened.

The disjunction of House and Senate introduces the central theme of this chapter: Divergent outcomes of House and presidential contests are only one manifestation of a much broader pattern of electoral disintegration. Indeed, the progressive dissociation of election results across both offices and election years is among the most striking and fundamental postwar electoral developments.[1]

At the level of individual voters, disintegration shows up as an increase in ticket splitting; surveys supply abundant evidence of citizens' increasing propensity to vote for candidates of different parties for different offices during the postwar period (Wattenberg 1990). At the level of election outcomes, disintegration shows up as a diminishing association between election results for different offices with overlapping constituencies and, for the same office, diminishing continuity from one election to the next. Election outcomes have become less predictable by either past (what happened last time) or present (what happens in coterminous elections) events. The outcomes of House elections, the special focus of this book, have become progressively detached from outcomes of elections for president, Senate, governor, and state legislative seats, as well as from each other and from elections in the same district across election years.

DIVIDED VOTERS

The proximate source of electoral disintegration is reasonably well established: a decline in partisanship and, more importantly, party loyalty

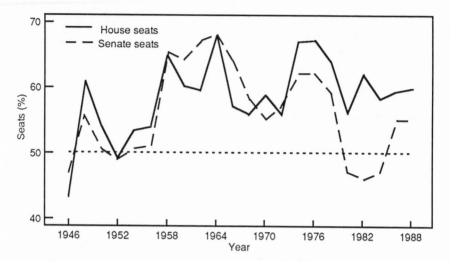

FIGURE 2.2 Democrats' Share of House and Senate Seats, 1946–1988

Note: The senators whose official affiliation was with other than the Democratic or Republican parties are treated as members of the party with whom they voted to organize.

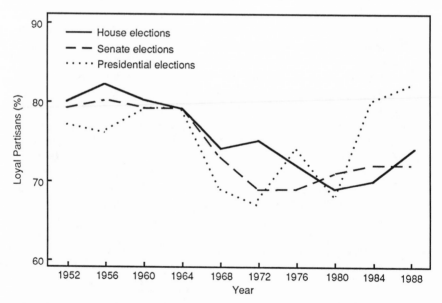

FIGURE 2.3 Party Loyalty Among Voters in House, Senate, and Presidential Elections, 1952–1988

among voters. The degree to which partisanship has declined is a matter of some controversy. If partisanship is measured as the proportion of citizens who claim allegiance to one of the major parties, excluding apoliticals and those who call themselves independents even though they admit, on subsequent questioning, to lean toward a party, data from the American National Election Studies show a decline in party identifiers from 74.4% of citizens in 1952 to 62.7% in 1988. If leaners are included among the partisans (as Keith et al. [1977] argue that, on behavioral grounds, they should be), the decline is considerably more modest, from 91.1% in 1952 to 87.8% in 1988 (Wattenberg 1990). Even this decline may be of little practical importance; because turnout among "pure" independents has fallen, the proportion of self-reported voters placing themselves in this category has not grown at all (Ornstein, Mann, and Malbin 1990:65).

Although the size of the independent fraction may be in question, there is no doubt whatever about the diminished loyalty of professed partisans and the increased propensity of voters in every partisan category to split their tickets. Figures 2.3 and 2.4 illustrate these trends graphically. Figure 2.3 traces changes in the percentage of House, Senate, and presidential electorates composed of loyal partisans—people voting for candidates of their professed party—since 1952. Partisan loyalty among House and Senate voters declined sharply between the first and second halves of this period. The proportion of loyalists among presidential voters fell in similar fashion until 1984 and 1988, when it rebounded above levels prevailing in the 1950s. This sharp exception to the general trend suggests that many survey respondents in the 1980s defined their partisanship by their presidential preference, a development with implications I shall consider in the concluding chapter. Figure 2.4 shows the growth in the proportion of the electorate that reports voting for House and presidential candidates, and House and Senate candidates, of different parties. The frequency of ticket splitting between these pairs of offices has nearly tripled since 1952.

The weakening of party loyalty and growth of ticket-splitting have contributed to a sizable increase in the heterogeneity of election results. District-level House election outcomes have become increasingly disconnected from those for other elective offices as well as from each other. The most commonly mentioned manifestation of this trend is the growth in the percentage of districts in which pluralities vote for presidential candidates of one party and House candidates of the other party, which is displayed in Figure 2.5; elections from the earlier New Deal period are included to show just how different the postwar pattern is. Not surprisingly, split results are more common in elections with lopsided presidential results (at least in the postwar period), but the

FIGURE 2.4 Ticket Splitting in Federal Elections, 1952–1988

coefficients estimated by the regression equation in Table 2.1 confirm that, assuming that the presidential candidates divide the vote evenly, the expected proportion of split results has risen from 14% to 34% since 1948.

The growing dissociation of House and presidential outcomes at the district level is sometimes read as the shrinking of presidential coattails. Certainly, if coattails are measured by the capacity of winning presidential candidates to pull their party's other candidates into office along with them, the data are reasonably persuasive: Presidential coattails have indeed atrophied. (I shall offer some additional evidence on this point in Chapter 5.) But other interpretations of the concept—it is by no means easy to pin down—and other methods of analysis leave the issue in some doubt, because different measures and methods support conflicting conclusions.[2] For example, significant coattail effects may appear

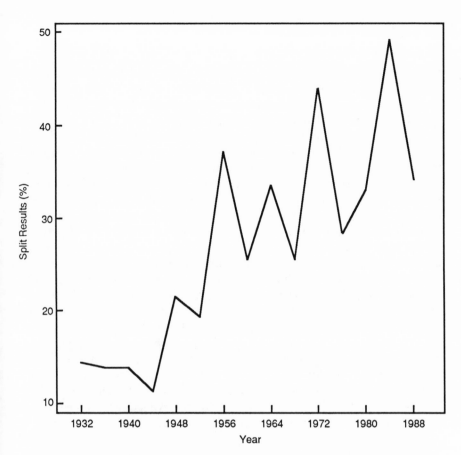

FIGURE 2.5 District-Level Split Results of House and Presidential Elections, 1932–1988

TABLE 2.1
Districts with Split Results for President and House, 1948–1988

Variable	
Intercept	12.16**
	(3.72)
Presidential vote: winner-loser (%)	.75**
	(.19)
Election year	1.81**
	(.49)
Adjusted R^2	.75
Durbin-Watson	2.23
Number of cases	11

**$p < .01$, one-tailed test.

Note: The dependent variable is the percentage of districts in which pluralities voted for a presidential candidate of one party and a House candidate of the other party; the values of "election year" are 1948 = 1, 1952 = 2, . . . 1988 = 11; standard errors of regression coefficients are in parentheses.

at the level of individual voters even when aggregate outcomes show little sign of coattails (Jacobson 1987b). And Richard Born argues that, "while split-party results have become more common, the power of coattails to move candidates' reelection percentages above or below their base level has stayed rather constant" (1984:76).

Such discrepant findings are commonly blamed on the enhanced power of incumbency: Successful presidential candidates may swing as many votes to their party as before, but the enlarged margin of safety enjoyed by House incumbents reduces the proportion of members whose seats are vulnerable to the swing (Born 1984; Mondak 1989). This follows logically from the conventional view of how the electoral value of incumbency has grown since 1946. I shall take issue with several aspects of this view in the next chapter. For present purposes, I need only point out that split results are almost as common in open House districts as in those contested by incumbents. In elections from 1968 to 1988, which follow the supposedly sharp increase in the incumbency advantage, 29.0% of all open-seat contests produced split results, compared to 35.0% of all incumbent-contested districts. The difference, while in the expected direction, falls short of statistical significance.[3] The large proportion of divided outcomes in recent elections cannot, then, be merely the consequence of an enhanced incumbency advantage. House votes may move with presidential votes as they have in the past, but other influences—and not just incumbency—have intervened to limit the impact of the presidential election on local election outcomes.

SPLIT RESULTS AMONG OTHER OFFICES

Evidence from elections for statewide offices reinforces the view that the trend toward electoral disaggregation is characteristic of the entire political system. House and Senate results have become increasingly disconnected regardless of House incumbency. Figure 2.6 plots the percentage of House seats won by the same party that won the state's Senate and gubernatorial contests against the election year. The decline in consistency is steep, and it is characteristic of both open and incumbent-contested seats and non-Southern as well as Southern districts.[4] In recent elections, a party has about the same chance of winning a given House seat in a state regardless of whether or not it wins the Senate or gubernatorial election in the state. In 1988, for example, Democrats took 61% of the House seat in states won by Democratic Senate candidates and 58% of the House seats in states won by Republican Senate candidates.

House results have also become distinct from state legislative outcomes. This is demonstrated by the probit equations in Table 2.2, which estimate the probability that a Democrat won the House election depending on

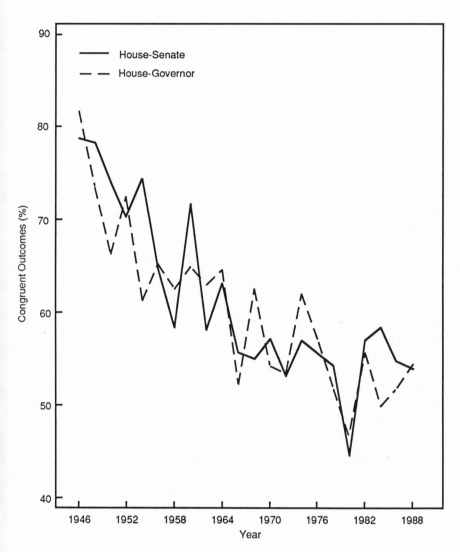

FIGURE 2.6 Congruency of Election Outcomes for House, Senate, and Governor, 1946–1988

TABLE 2.2

Probit Estimates of the Relationship Between House and State Legislative Elections, 1946–1988

Variable	All Seats	Open Seats
Intercept	−1.862***	−2.002***
	(0.079)	(0.239)
Seats won by Democrats in the lower house of the state legislature (%)	.037***	.039***
	(.001)	(.004)
Election year	.059***	.068***
	(.007)	(.021)
Election year × state legislative seats won by Democrats (%)	−.0011***	−.0014***
	(.0001)	(.0004)
Log likelihood	−5,507	−594
Number of cases	9,360	1,004

***p < .001, one-tailed test.

Note: The coefficients are maximum likelihood estimates; the dependent variable is 1 if the Democrat won the seat, 0 if the Republican won the seat; the values of "election year" are 1946 = 1, 1948 = 2, . . . 1988 = 22; standard errors are in parentheses.

the percentage of seats won by Democrats in the lower House of the legislature, the election year, and the interaction between the two. The significant negative coefficient on the interaction terms reveals the diminishing connection between the two types of elections. The decline is substantial; the coefficients indicate that the statistical effect of state legislative outcomes has fallen by nearly two-thirds in the postwar period. Assuming an initial probability of around .5, for example, a 10 percentage-point difference in state legislative victories was associated with a .14 difference in the probability of a Democratic House victory in 1946, only a .05 difference by 1988. And note that the decline is just as great when open seats alone are examined; the change cannot, therefore, be blamed on any augmentation of the House incumbency advantage.

Electoral disaggregation is not confined to comparisons involving the House. State-level results for simultaneous Senate and gubernatorial contests are no longer related.[5] The number of divided state governments rose from eleven in 1946 to a record high thirty-two in 1988; statistically, partisan control of the governorship and state legislature have been completely unrelated in recent years (Fiorina 1990). In 1988, the statewide vote percentages for George Bush and the Republican Senate candidate were not significantly correlated; Republican Senate candidates won in eleven of the twenty-five states (44%) that Bush won and in three of the eight states (38%) won by Dukakis, an insignificant difference (Jacobson 1989). Wherever one looks, the association between election results for different offices with overlapping constituencies has diminished, often to insignificance.

Naturally, electoral disintegration is a special source of frustration for Republicans, because it has denied them the traditional rewards of trickle-down politics. If straight-ticket voting were still the custom and the choice were determined by the top of the ticket, Republicans would by now be in control almost everywhere, not least in Congress. The disaggregation of election outcomes across offices has allowed the Democrats to survive, even prosper, at other electoral levels despite nominating a string of presidential losers.

The demise of trickle-down electoral politics has hurt Republicans in another more specific way as well. Republican presidential victories have done little to strengthen the Republican party in the states. Democrats continue to control a majority of state legislatures and governorships. Democratic predominance in state legislatures—they held 60% of state legislative seats after 1988—is especially important, because it gives the party a deeper pool of talent from which to draw congressional candidates. The importance of fielding experienced candidates in House elections is documented fully in Chapter 4; the point to note here is that state legislatures are by far the most important source of experienced House candidates, and Republican presidential victories have so far failed to strengthen the Republican party in the lower offices that are the most common stepping-stones to Congress.

Finally, it is worth emphasizing that widespread dissociation of election outcomes across a range of state and federal offices means that explanations of divided control based on specific structural features of House elections, such as the incumbency advantage or gerrymandered districts, are bound to be incomplete and may even be unnecessary. It is not, after all, easy to conjure up similar structural explanations for divided outcomes across all the other levels.

THE GROWING HETEROGENEITY OF HOUSE ELECTION RESULTS

Not only have House elections become increasingly detached from elections for other offices, but they have become increasingly detached from each other as well. Interelection vote swings have become more variable across districts; district-level results show less consistency from one election to the next. These phenomena are closely related: If swings were completely uniform across districts, then district results in the second election could be predicted with perfect accuracy from the results of the first election once the swing was known.

A simple measure of the variability of swings across districts is the standard deviation of the swing, with the swing defined as the change in the percentage share of the district two-party vote won by a party from one election to the next. The greater the standard deviation of the interelection vote swing, the less uniform electoral trends are across House districts. Consistency across time is determined by the accuracy with which election results in one election predict results in the next election. This can be measured by regressing the vote in the current election on the vote in the previous election and examining the standard error of the regression (SER).

In practice, the two methods produce results that are nearly identical. To see why, consider the regression equation from which the SERs are calculated:

$$DV_t = a + bDV_{t-1} \qquad (1)$$

where DV is the Democrats' share of the two-party vote, t indicates the election year, and a is the intercept and b the regression coefficient. The standard deviation of the interelection vote swing is equivalent to the SER of

$$DV_t - DV_{t-1} = a \qquad (2)$$

In this equation the constant, a, gives the mean swing and the SER is the standard deviation of the variation around it. When $b = 1$, the SERs of equations 1 and 2 are identical. Estimated b's for the twenty-two postwar election years range from .79 to 1.01, with a mean of .93 and standard deviation of .06. Hence these two measures of variability are usually very close. Both of them are shown in Figure 2.7. The entries in this figure are based on analysis of all stable (non-redistricted) districts in each election year; election years ending in 2 are excluded because they hold relatively few stable districts.[6]

Figure 2.7 shows that consistency of elections over time and across House districts has decreased substantially since 1946 and, as expected, the two trends are nearly identical (r = .995). But growth in the electoral value of incumbency, to be examined at length in the next chapter, would by itself be expected to increase the variability. Both the "sophomore surge"—the gain in votes enjoyed by candidates running as incumbents for the first time—and "retirement slump"—the shift of votes away from a party when its incumbents retire—work in the same direction for both parties regardless of national partisan trends. In 1974, for example, the average Republican freshman actually won a larger share of votes than he had in 1972 despite the large national swing to

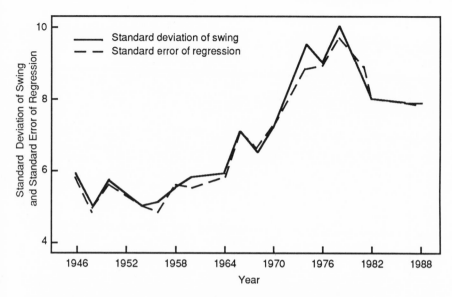

FIGURE 2.7 Growing Heterogeneity of House Election Results, 1946–1988

the Democrats. Thus as the sophomore surge and retirement slump grow, so should the variability of district-level results.

The data presented in Figure 2.8, however, indicate that the increase in electoral volatility is not confined to open seats or to those held by first-term incumbents. The entries are SERs from iterations of equation 1. (Again, I have included only stable districts and have dropped election years ending in 2.) The figure compares results for two types of elections: those for open seats, which should be the most volatile, and those involving nonfreshman incumbents, which are not affected by the sophomore surge or retirement slump and therefore should be the least volatile. The figure shows that volatility has increased significantly for both categories.[7]

Open-seat outcomes have always been less accurately predicted from past results, and predictive error has grown, albeit irregularly, over time. This is, to some degree, a consequence of the increased retirement slump (both parties losing a larger chunk of votes when the incumbency advantage is lost regardless of national tides); but this is by no means most of the explanation, because the SERs show a similar increase when open seats are separated by party and the SERs are averaged for the election year. The central point, however, is that continuity between elections has diminished even for seats not subject to the confounding forces generated by an increased incumbency advantage: those held by veteran incumbents. Thus the increased electoral value of incumbency

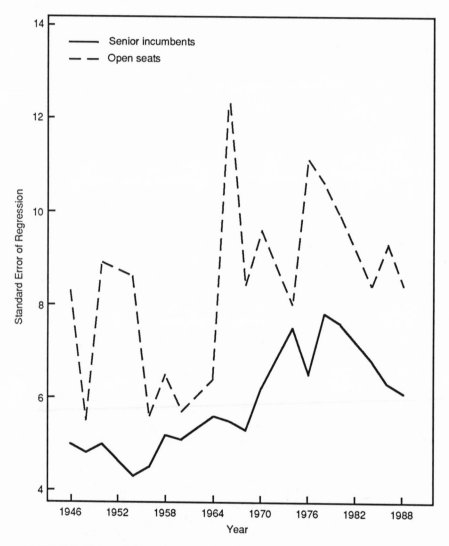

FIGURE 2.8 Heterogeneity of House Election Results for Open Seats and Senior Incumbents, 1946–1988

TABLE 2.3
Incidence of Surge and Decline, 1946–1966 and 1968–1988 (in percentages)

	1946–1966	1968–1988
Seats switching party control:		
that had switched party control in the previous election	35.7	8.4
	(403)	(322)
that were retaken in the next election	40.0	15.6
	(360)	(173)

Note: The number of cases is in parentheses.

cannot by itself account for the increased volatility of House election results.

SURGE AND DECLINE

Yet another manifestation of electoral disintegration in House elections is a sharp change in the way partisan tides affect the turnover of House seats. During the first half of the postwar period, close partisan competition tended to be concentrated in a particular subset of House seats. That is, the seats that changed hands in one election were much more likely to change hands in the next election, and, in parallel fashion, the seats that changed party control in the current election were much more likely to have switched in the previous election as well. Since the mid-1960s, however, partisan competition has been dispersed across a larger number of districts, and the likelihood that a seat switches party control in two successive elections is much smaller.

Tides of "surge and decline" (Campbell 1960) still occur; the more seats a party wins in one election, the more seats it is likely to lose in the next election. The difference is that the *individual* seats lost in the "decline" are far less likely to be seats won in the prior "surge" than they were before. The evidence is in Table 2.3. Before 1968, 40.0% of the seats that changed party hands were recaptures of seats taken by the other party in the previous election; since then, only 15.6% of seat switches fall into this category. Similarly, before 1968, the party recaptured 35.7% of the seats taken from it in the previous election; since then, it has immediately retaken only 8.4% of the seats it has lost.

This change reflects the dramatic improvement in the electoral fortunes of freshman members of the House. From 1946 through 1966, more than one-third (35.9%, to be precise, including freshman members elected in special elections) of the members who entered the House by taking a seat from the other party were defeated in their first reelection bid. Since 1968, only 8.5% of members in this category have lost after one term. The sharp decline in the electoral vulnerability of newly elected members is usually taken as evidence for an enlarged incumbency advantage; but it is also indicative of a more disaggregated, disjointed electoral process in which district-level outcomes are shaped to a much greater degree by the interaction of local factors with national tides than by the national tides alone. And it means that more senior incumbents now hold a larger share of seats lost to contrary partisan tides.

SOURCES OF DISAGGREGATION

Partisan disintegration, then, is characteristic of the entire electoral system during the postwar period. Its immediate source is the decline in party loyalty among voters. This, in turn, is usually traced to two other major developments. One is the increased ability of candidates and elected officials to communicate directly with voters without relying on party organizations or a partisan press to get the message across. The advent of television as a campaign medium and the growth of resources available to elected officials to communicate with constituents— most notoriously the office, travel, and communications allowances enjoyed by members of the House and Senate—are the most prominent developments of this sort. The more sophisticated technology of travel and communication has clearly made it easier for candidates with the requisite resources to establish personal ties with voters and thus to build personal, as opposed to impersonally partisan, electoral coalitions.

Of greater importance, however, have been changes in the utility of party cues to voters. As long as electoral politics were given focus by New Deal issues, partisan lines were reasonably clear: Democrats were for New Deal policies, Republicans opposed them. The party label thus gave voters adequate information for expressing their preferences on the dominant political issues. Once the major New Deal institutions were firmly in place and no longer threatened by Republicans (the Eisenhower administration made the decisive contribution here), other divisions came to the fore—over civil rights, the Great Society welfare programs, the Vietnam War, energy and environment, and "social issues" such as abortion rights, crime, and the bounds of acceptable social behavior— that did not divide the parties either consistently or predictably. The party label became less informative and thus less useful to voters as a shorthand cue for predicting what elected officials would do once in office. Information about individual candidates became more important.

Among members of Congress, the motive—establishing a personal electoral base to facilitate reelection—has probably been there since the beginning of this century. Postwar technological innovations provided the means. But the opportunity was created by partisan incoherence.

Some indirect evidence for the primary role of politics—as opposed to technology—in explaining the decline of party loyalty and straight-ticket voting can be found in every figure in this chapter. Note that, by almost every measure, the electoral fragmentation peaked in the late 1970s and then declined somewhat—though remaining well above immediate post-war levels—in the 1980s. The opportunities provided by communication technologies and resources have continued to grow, but as political lines clarified during the Reagan administration, so did electoral coherence. With party labels more informative, voters have been more disposed to use them.

The combination of technology and politics contributed jointly to a growing electoral focus on individual candidates. Putting candidates front and center fragments electoral competition and shrinks the national component of electoral politics, because the variation across districts among individual candidates—and, even more, among the choices presented by pairs of candidates—is considerably greater than the variation across districts in the impact of partisan tides.

In House elections, the most prominent sign of the growing importance of individual candidates at the expense of partisan loyalties was a rise in the electoral advantages conferred by incumbency. Schematically, House incumbents took advantage of the opportunity provided by newly available resources for communicating with constituents and the diminished value of party cues to voters (and hence their greater willingness to base their vote on the characteristics of individual candidates) to build personal coalitions that transcended partisanship. The details of just how they have carried this off are still hotly contested in the literature (Johannes and McAdams 1981; Fiorina 1981b; Jacobson 1987b; Fiorina and Rivers 1989), but no one questions that a significant move in this direction occurred.

I shall argue in the next chapter that the incumbency advantage has been exaggerated and, in important respects, misinterpreted. For now, I wish only to point out that, while the declining importance of partisanship and the growth of a more candidate-centered electoral politics may have made it easier for House incumbents to hold seats in the face of contrary partisan tides, it should also open the way for parties to win seats that loyally partisan electorates once denied them. And, indeed, more seats did become available to both parties. Fewer stable House districts were monopolized by one party during the 1970s (240 of 361, or 66.5%) than during the 1950s (303 of 394, or 76.9%), and the difference is statistically significant ($Z = 3.18$, $p < .01$).[8] This remains true even when the analysis is confined to seats outside the South (64.2% monopolized in the 1970s, compared with 71.8% in the 1950s, $Z = 1.97$, $p < .05$). But, reflecting the dispersal of partisan competition, a smaller proportion of switched districts switched more than once in the 1970s (21 of 121, 17.3%) than in the 1950s (34 of 91, or 37.4%); again, the difference is significant (Z = 4.35, p < .001).

If, despite an increased incumbency advantage, more House seats are up for grabs, partisan competition can hardly be viewed as declining, at least between the 1950s and the 1970s.[9] Furthermore, incumbents do not live forever; with more seats open to both parties, long-run electoral benefits should accrue to whichever party's candidates are able to make the most of their expanded opportunities.[10]

NOTES

1. Walter Dean Burnham, who has published the most work on "partisan decomposition," argues that it "was a dominant leitmotif of political change in the United States across the last century" (1985:234), with the early New Deal producing the only contrary trend. But even Burnham's data show the trend to be strongest during the postwar period (1985:235).

2. See, for example, Burnham (1975); Edwards (1980); Calvert and Ferejohn (1983); Born (1984); Ferejohn and Calvert (1984); and Mondak (1989).

3. Using a difference of proportions test, Z = 1.89, which does not exceed the p < .05 threshold for statistical significance in a two-tailed test.

4. Regression equations for data from all of these subcategories produced significant negative coefficients on "election year." The slopes do not vary by incumbency status or statewide office, but they are steeper for the South than for states outside the South.

5. The partisan outcomes of contests for senator and governor were significantly related (according to chi-squared tests of cross tabulations) in all election years from 1946 through 1960 and in *no* election year since then. Even when all contests for the 1962–1988 period are aggregated into a single data set, outcomes are statistically independent; split results occur in 45.2% of the cases, compared to 18.9% in the earlier period.

6. While technically advisable, excluding the redrawn districts and the years ending in "2" makes little difference; nearly the same results appear if districts with new boundaries (but otherwise identifiable as covering most of a previous district, so that DV_{t-1} can be observed) are included in the analysis.

7. The equation for open seats is

$$SER = 6.89 + .132 \times \text{election year}$$
$$\quad\quad (0.85) \quad (.065)$$

$$\bar{R}^2 = .16$$

The equation for nonfreshman incumbents, which was estimated by generalized least squares because the Durbin-Watson statistic from ordinary least squares indicated serial correlation in the errors, is

$$\text{SER} = 4.51 + .113 \times \text{election year}$$
$$\qquad\quad (0.45) \quad (.033)$$

$$\bar{R}^2 = .67, \text{ rho} = .40$$

8. These are the only full postwar decades in which a large majority of districts maintained stable boundaries. Here and elsewhere, I define decades by reapportionment cycles. The 1960s, for example, include election years from 1962 through 1970.

9. For the first four elections of the 1980s (1982 through 1988), partisan turnover was well below previous decades. Part of the reason is that the only election for the decade showing a strong partisan tide was 1982, which came at the beginning. That is not the whole story, however; see Chapters 3 and 6.

10. Although this book is concerned almost exclusively with House elections, a brief discussion of trends in postwar Senate elections is useful for summarizing some of the points of this chapter. The decline of partisan loyalty and the spread of partisan competition have left both parties with a chance to win statewide offices virtually everywhere. After the 1988 election, twenty-two states were represented by one senator from each party; thirty-one states have chosen senators from both parties in elections since 1978. Of the remaining states, all but two—Hawaii and Massachusetts—have elected governors of the party opposite their senators' during the past decade.

The changes that opened up new opportunities for parties to compete in regions once dominated by the opposition have been thoroughly exploited by statewide candidates. Incumbency was no barrier to a Republican takeover of the Senate, but neither did it help them retain it; Republicans lost their majority in 1986 when seven Republican incumbents were defeated despite, in most cases, a very large financial advantage. Recent Senate elections illustrate the potential for surprise that fickle electorates and candidate-centered electoral politics have created.

3

After the Primal Scream: The Incumbency Advantage Revisited

The postwar electoral trend that has attracted the most scholarly attention, as well as the most blame for stifling competition and for keeping Republicans from winning a "fair" share of seats in the House of Representatives, is, of course, the increased electoral advantage enjoyed by incumbent members. Far too much attention, by some lights: "I am convinced," Charles O. Jones wrote in a 1981 review essay, "that one more article demonstrating that House incumbents tend to win reelection will induce a spontaneous primal scream among all congressional scholars across the nation" (1981:458).

In blithe disregard of Professor Jones's warning, the stream of articles examining the incumbency advantage continues unabated.[1] Part of the reason is that scholars continue to disagree about how to measure as well as how to explain the phenomenon. But the issue retains its interest, I think, largely because of its deeper implications for the political system. If incumbents have become so entrenched that their only serious electoral worry is a felony indictment, the partisan makeup of the House can respond feebly, if at all, to changes in voters' preferences, and a fundamental pillar of representative democracy is missing. On a more mundane level, Republicans may indeed be justified in thinking that the structural advantages associated with incumbency have prevented them from winning their rightful share of House seats, and divided government is open to a simple structural explanation. If, however, the advantages of incumbency have been exaggerated, or if contrary trends have emerged, the threat to democracy has been overstated; Republicans will have to find another explanation for their failure to do better in House elections, and scholars will have to entertain other explanations for divided government.

In this chapter, I examine changes in the incumbency advantage yet again, but with, I think, more skepticism than is customary and considerably more attention to the neglected downside of the enlarged incumbency advantage: the parties' diminished ability to retain seats when the incumbent dies or retires. My central point is that changes in the incumbency advantage, such as they are, have not created a "permanent House" and cannot account for Republicans' inability to win more House seats or, by extension, divided party control of the federal government.

MEASURING THE HOUSE INCUMBENCY ADVANTAGE

To examine changes in the electoral advantage conferred by incumbency, one must first measure it. Scholars have proposed a variety of yardsticks, and all of them indicate that significant change has occurred. Different measures, however, reveal rather different patterns of change. Fortunately, discrepant findings are in this instance fruitful rather than frustrating, because they compel reexamination of questions that lead to deeper insights into what has happened.

Two obvious measures of electoral prowess are the ability to win votes and the ability to win elections. Other things equal, if the advantages of incumbency have grown, incumbents should be winning more votes and more elections. Curiously, neither of these unadorned measures attracted much systematic attention in the initial burst of scholarship on the incumbency advantage. I shall begin with consideration of votes and, after a discussion of other indices of the incumbency advantage, finish with a discussion of electoral victories.

By the simple criterion of winning votes, the value of House incumbency has increased in linear fashion since 1946. Figure 3.1 displays the rise in the average share of the major-party vote won by House incumbents over this period. Regression of vote shares on the election year indicates that the value in votes of House incumbency grew by .41 percentage points from one election to the next during the postwar period.[2] In 1946, the average House incumbent could expect to win 59.3% of the two-party vote in contested elections; in 1988, the incumbent's expected vote was 67.8%, an increase of 8.5 percentage points.

David Mayhew's seminal article (1974b) on the "vanishing marginals" also used vote shares as primary data, but Mayhew measured the incumbency advantage by the percentage of incumbents whose vote left their grip on the district in doubt: the marginals. The two thresholds of marginality commonly found in the literature are 55% and 60% of the vote. Winning candidates who fall short of the threshold are considered to hold marginal seats; those who exceed it are considered safe from electoral threats. Over time, the percentage of marginal incumbents has declined in tandem by both criteria (they are correlated at r = .93);

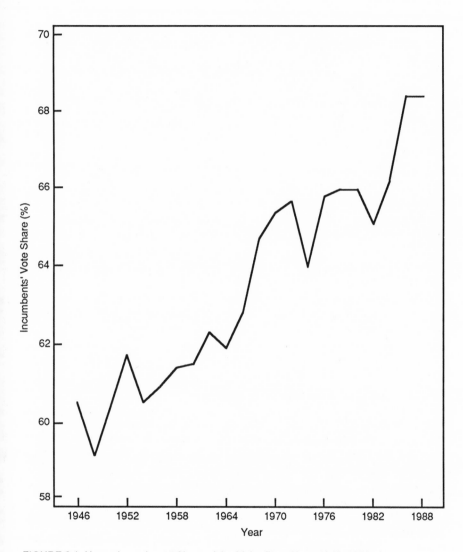

FIGURE 3.1 House Incumbents' Share of the Major-Party Vote, 1946–1988

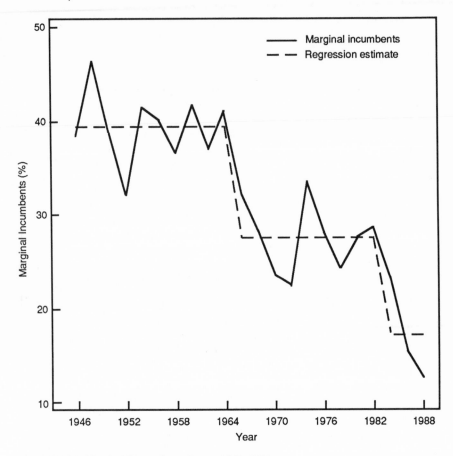

FIGURE 3.2 Marginal House Incumbents, 1946–1988

either tells the same story. But unlike the rise in vote shares, the change was not gradual.

Figure 3.2 shows that the percentage of marginal incumbents (here using the 60% criterion) decreased as their average vote share increased (of course, the two measures are strongly, and negatively, related: r = −.96), but suggests that the change came in two large steps rather than in numerous smaller increments. It also shows a fitted regression line estimated using dummy variables representing 1966 through 1982 and 1984 through 1988; the regression results reported in Table 3.1 show this model to fit the data better than a model estimating the change as a linear decline. Through 1964 we observe fluctuations but no trend. In the late 1960s the proportion of marginal seats dropped to a lower plateau, where it remained until a further drop in the late 1980s. The

TABLE 3.1
Change in Percentage of Marginal House Seats, 1946–1988

Variable	(1)	(2)
Intercept	44.7***	39.2***
	(2.1)	(1.2)
Election year	−1.2***	
	(0.2)	
1966–1982		−11.8***
		(1.8)
1984–1988		−22.2***
		(2.6)
Adjusted R²	.71	.81
Durbin-Watson	1.43	2.15
Number of cases	22	22

***p < .001, one-tailed test.

Note: Dependent variable is the percentage of incumbents winning with less than 60% of the two-party vote; the values of "election year" are 1946 = 1, 1948 = 2, . . . 1988 = 22; "1966–1982" and "1984–1988" are dummy variables that take the value of 1 if the year falls within the specified range, 0 otherwise; the standard errors of the regression coefficients are in parentheses.

coefficients indicate that the expected proportion of marginal incumbents dropped from 39% for 1946–1964 to 27% for 1966–1982 and to 17% for the most recent three elections.

The timing of these two shifts coincides closely with the attention paid to House incumbency. The first stimulated the extensive "vanishing marginals" literature in political science. The second underlies the recent spate of handwringing among pundits and (Republican) politicians over the disappearance of electoral competition in the House.

As John Alford and David Brady (1988) note explicitly, and earlier students of the incumbency advantage recognized implicitly, the incumbents' mean vote percentage, and other indices based upon it, do not provide unambiguous measures of the incumbency advantage per se. Incumbents could, on average, win a large share of the vote simply because they represent districts where *any* candidate of their party would get a large share of the vote. Their margin might derive not from incumbency, but from district partisanship. The electoral value of incumbency per se is determined by how much better incumbents do than would candidates of their party who are not incumbents.

Several measures of the difference in votes that incumbency itself makes have thus been developed. Robert Erikson (1972) and Albert Cover and David Mayhew (1981) examine changes over time in the "sophomore surge" and "retirement slump"—respectively, the additional share of votes a party typically wins when its candidate first seeks reelection as an incumbent and loses when the seat becomes open. Alford and Brady (1988) average the two into a "slurge" to compute their index of the value, in votes, of incumbency.

Andrew Gelman and Gary King (1989) demonstrate that the sophomore surge, retirement slump, and, by extension, "slurge" are distorted by selection bias and propose an alternative technique. To compute an unbiased measure, they regress the Democrat's share of the two-party vote on the Democrat's vote in the previous election, the party holding the seat, and incumbency (which takes a value of 1 if the Democratic candidate is an incumbent, -1 if the Republican is an incumbent, 0 if the seat is open). The coefficient on the incumbency variable estimates the value (in percentage of votes) of incumbency for each election year. In practice, all of these indices show very similar patterns of change in the value of incumbency; the principal difference is that Gelman and King's measure gives incumbency a slightly higher value. Figure 3.3 shows how the coefficient on their incumbency variable has changed since 1946.[3] Observe once again a dramatic jump in the electoral value of incumbency, so measured, between 1964 and 1966.

The contrast between the gradual increase in the share of votes incumbents win (Figure 3.1) and the much sharper step increase between 1964 and 1966 in the value of incumbency measured by the other indices (Figures 3.2 and 3.3) is puzzling. According to Gelman and King's measure, the value of incumbency jumped from 3.6% to 11.6% of the vote between the two elections; according to the retirement slump, it went from 3.1% to 8.4%. It is no small irony, then, that 1966 was in fact a particularly *bad* year for (Democratic) incumbents. It is difficult to understand how, if the advantages conferred by incumbency really did increase so dramatically between 1964 and 1966, forty incumbents still managed to *lose* in 1966. The only postwar years worse for incumbents than 1966 were 1946 (forty-eight defeated), 1948 (sixty-seven), 1964 (forty-five), and 1974 (forty-one). And how could there be such a sharp increase in the other indices of the incumbency advantage between 1964 and 1966 when the mean share of votes won by incumbents increased only 0.9 percentage points?

The answer to the first question is that the connection between the value of incumbency measured in vote margins and its value measured in the more basic currency of wins and losses is not nearly as strong as scholars initially assumed. I will have more to say about this later. The answer to the second question is that, as Alford and Brady (1988) point out, measures such as Gelman and King's regression coefficient or the retirement slump vary with changes in two distinct variables. One is the value, in votes, of incumbency per se, what Alford and Brady

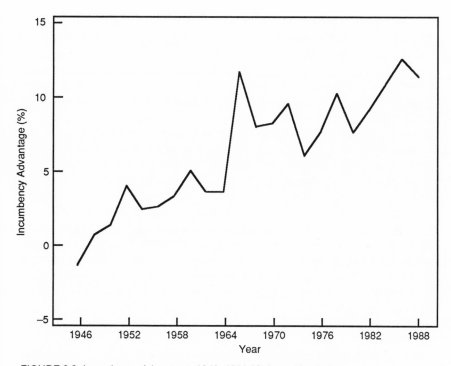

FIGURE 3.3 Incumbency Advantage, 1946–1988 (Gelman-King Index)

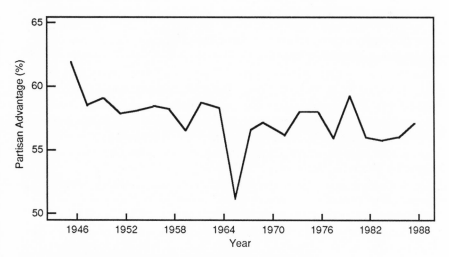

FIGURE 3.4 Partisan Advantage in House Elections, 1946–1988

Note: Partisan advantage = mean vote for incumbents − Gelman-King index of the incumbency advantage.

call the personal value of incumbency. The other is value, in votes, of the seat to the party holding it independent of incumbency. Alford and Brady propose estimating the party's advantage by subtracting the personal value of incumbency from the mean share of votes won by incumbents. That is, the incumbent's share of votes, minus the vote advantage conferred by incumbency, equals the vote advantage enjoyed by the party holding the seat independent of incumbency.

The results of this calculation, using Gelman and King's unbiased measure of the incumbency advantage, appear in Figure 3.4. Notice first that, as the value of incumbency has increased, the partisan component of the incumbency advantage has declined. That is, over time, a party's expected vote in the seats it currently holds, independent of the incumbency effect, has shrunk. The coefficient estimated by regressing this variable on the election year indicates that the party's expected vote, absent incumbency, fell from 58.8% to 55.6% over the postwar period.[4] Notice also that 1966 is an extreme outlier. The sharp increase in the incumbency advantage recorded between 1964 and 1966 by the usual measures did not arise from incumbents winning a significantly larger share of votes than before, but rather from parties doing dramatically worse in seats that became open.[5]

These results help explain how the vote value of incumbency could appear to increase sharply in an election in which an unusually large number of incumbents lost and the average incumbent's vote share increased very little. The results also imply that House incumbents have not derived as much electoral benefit from the rise of the incumbency advantage as the usual indices might suggest, because the rise has been offset, in part, by a decrease in the partisan component of the typical incumbent's vote margin.

A further implication of Figure 3.4 is that, if vote margins measure competitiveness, *as competition for seats held by incumbents has declined, competition for open seats has increased.* This is no coincidence, of course. Both changes reflect the trend toward a more personal, candidate-centered, electoral politics. The same conditions that have made it possible for incumbents to enhance their personal hold on the district have made it more difficult for either party to monopolize a constituency. Because this point has often been overlooked by scholars mesmerized by the growth of incumbents' vote margins, and because it has direct bearing on arguments concerning the structural barriers to Republican advances in the House, it requires further elaboration.

COMPETITION FOR OPEN HOUSE SEATS

Competition for open seats has, by a variety of measures, increased since 1946. Most of the change occurred during the decade following the war. For example, Figure 3.5 shows that the mean vote for the party holding an open seat trended downward through the mid-1960s, though it has since rebounded somewhat (note once again that 1966 is an extreme outlier). Figure 3.6 indicates that the proportion of marginal open seats (by the < 60% criterion) nearly doubled between the late 1940s and the late 1950s and has subsequently remained at around 60%. Figure 3.7 reveals a modest upward trend in the proportion of open seats that switched party control, although the change has not been at all smooth. Still, the difference between the first and second halves of the postwar period is significant: From 1946 through 1964, 20.3% of open House seats changed party hands; since then, 26.5% of open seats have switched party control. The difference is significant at $p < .05$.

Although it may have become more difficult to defeat incumbents— I will consider how much harder below—it has become easier to take seats from the opposition once those seats become open. Thus if the changes in House competition have really made it more difficult for a party to reap the benefits of a favorable trend in any single election year (by no means a certainty, as we shall see in Chapter 5), they have also made it easier for a party on the rise to accumulate seats over a series of elections as incumbents exit and their seats are thrown open. More specifically, if Democratic incumbency limited Republican gains in any one election, the greater opportunity to win open seats should have produced gradual Republican gains—if, that is, the incumbency advantage is the true explanation for the House Republicans' inability to match Republican gains elsewhere.

Table 3.2 shows what has actually occurred. The table lists the percentage of open seats that Democrats and Republicans were able to take from each other from 1946 to 1966 and from 1968 to 1988; the second period covers the era of Republican presidential hegemony. Both parties have increased their ability to win seats from the opposition, but Democrats have outdone Republicans. Since 1968, they have taken 27.6% of Republican open seats while losing 19.9% of their own. Naturally, the Democratic majority had more open seats to defend. However, even in strictly numerical terms, Democrats have taken more open seats from Republicans (62) than Republicans have taken from Democrats (60) since 1968. The parties have broken exactly even in the new seats created by redistricting in which neither or both parties fielded incumbent candidates (31 each).

Analysis of changes in the district partisan vote advantage, computed as before by subtracting the vote advantage attributed to incumbency from the mean vote for incumbents, indicates that, if anything, the loosening of partisan ties has created more problems for Republicans than for Democrats. The equations in Table 3.3 regress the vote advantage enjoyed by the party holding the seat on the election year, controlling

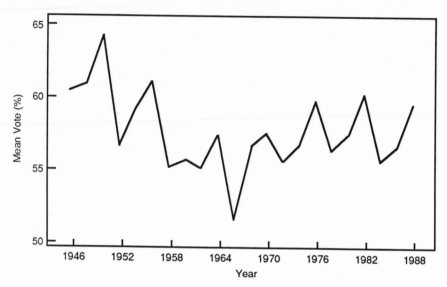

FIGURE 3.5 Mean Vote for Party Holding Open House Seat, 1946–1988

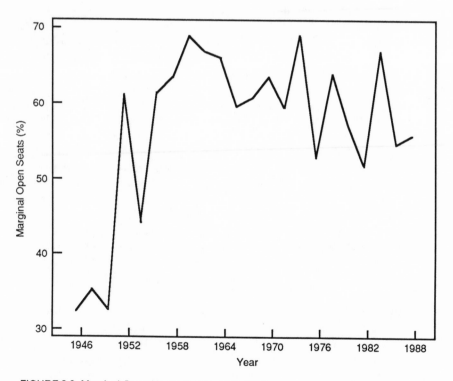

FIGURE 3.6 Marginal Open House Seats, 1946–1988

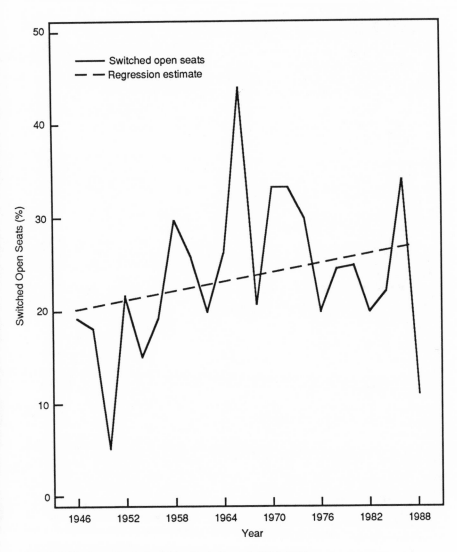

FIGURE 3.7 Open Seats Switching Party Control, 1946–1988

TABLE 3.2
Open Seats Changing Party Control, 1946–1988 (in percentages)

	Democrats' Seats	Republicans' Seats
1946–1966	16.1	22.5
	(273)	(244)
1968–1988	19.9	27.6
	(301)	(225)

Note: Includes general and special elections for open seats; the number of cases from which percentages were calculated are in parentheses.

TABLE 3.3
Change in Expected Party Vote When a House Seat Becomes Open, 1946–1988

Variable	Democrats' Seats	Republicans' Seats
Intercept	61.87***	58.00***
	(1.24)	(1.51)
Election year	−.21*	−.23*
	(.09)	(.12)
Seat swing to Democrats	.45***	−.25*
	(.08)	(.10)
Adjusted R^2	.60	.28
Durbin-Watson	1.84	1.45
Number of cases	22	22

*p < .05, one-tailed test.
***p < .001, one-tailed test.

Note: The dependent variable is the average incumbents' share of the two-party vote minus the value of incumbency according to the Gelman-King measure; the values of "election year" are 1946 = 1, 1948 = 2, . . . 1988 = 22; the "seat swing to Democrats" is the change in the percentage of seats won by Democrats from the previous election; the standard errors of the regression coefficients are in parentheses.

for national tides (measured by the change in percentage of House seats held by the Democrats). The value in votes of holding a seat has declined significantly for both parties, by about the same magnitude. However, the intercepts suggest that the change has been more troublesome for Republicans than for Democrats, because their partisan margin was almost 4 percentage points lower to begin with. The coefficients indicate that, assuming neutral national tides, the Democrats' typical partisan margin fell from 61.7% to 57.3% while the Republicans' margin fell from 57.8% to 53.0% over the postwar period. Absent incumbency, Republicans have maintained a distinctly lower margin of control over their House seats (though the coefficients on national tides suggest that Democrats have suffered more from tidal swings than have Republicans). Combining this with increasingly fickle district electorates (see Chapter 2), we begin to understand why Republicans have found it more difficult to hold onto seats when incumbents have retired in recent years.

It is clear from this evidence that incumbency cannot, by itself, explain why Republicans have not done better in House elections. Despite the general decline in a party's electoral advantage in the seats it holds, Republicans have made very little overall progress through open seats. And it is not for want of opportunity: Only 26 of the 260 Democrats holding seats in the House as of January 1, 1990, had been in the House prior to 1968; more than half (140) had first been elected in 1980 or later. This was also true of 110 of the 175 House Republicans. Alarm about an ossified, unchanging House seems downright silly when a solid majority of its members have been in office during only the Reagan and Bush administrations.

WINNING AND LOSING

Initially, the scholars transfixed by the vanishing marginals overlooked the point that the bottom line is not marginality or shares of votes, but winning or losing. It was simply assumed that wider margins of victory should make incumbents less vulnerable to defeat. Regardless of vote margins, however, incumbents did not really enjoy a fundamental gain in electoral advantage if they did not improve their chances of *winning* any given election. An overview of changes in the incumbency advantage measured by this standard is provided by Figure 3.8, which traces the percentage of successful incumbents across postwar House elections.

Clearly, House incumbents were much more vulnerable in the late 1940s than they are now. The 1946 and 1948 elections produced two huge electoral tides, Republicans defeating forty-five incumbents and adding 56 seats in 1946, Democrats defeating sixty-seven incumbents and adding 75 seats in 1948. No changes of comparable magnitude have

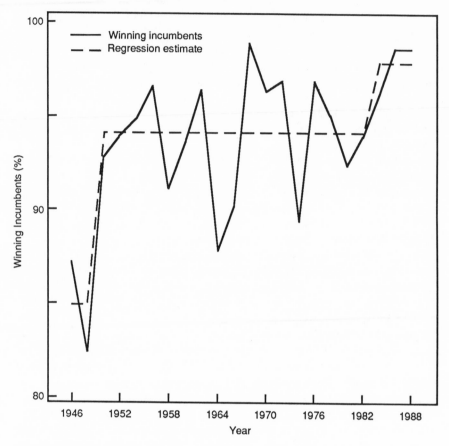

FIGURE 3.8 Electoral Success of House Incumbents, 1946–1988

taken place since. During the next three decades, however, while incumbents' electoral margins were, by every other measure, growing substantially, there was no significant increase in the proportion of incumbents winning reelection to the House. Only in the 1980s did incumbents' reelection rates surpass those of the 1950s.

The regression equations in Table 3.4 serve to document these points. Treating the change as a two-step sequence—the steps occurring between 1948 and 1950 and between 1982 and 1984—produces a much better fit to the data than assuming a linear increase in incumbents' electoral success (compare the first and second columns—the second equation is the source of the trend line in Figure 3.8). Indeed, the linear equation produces a positive, statistically significant coefficient only when 1946 and 1948 are included. The coefficient on time remains substantively

TABLE 3.4
Change in Percentage of Winning House Incumbents, 1946-1988

Variable	(1)	(2)
Intercept	89.6***	84.7***
	(1.6)	(2.2)
Election year	.35**	
	(.12)	
1966-1982		9.3***
		(2.2)
1984-1988		13.0***
		(2.7)
Adjusted R²	.26	.52
Durbin-Watson	1.75	2.21
Number of cases	22	22

**p < .01, one-tailed test.
***p < .001, one-tailed test.

Note: The dependent variable is the percentage of winning incumbents; the values of "election year" are 1946 = 1, 1948 = 2, . . . 1988 = 22; "1966-1982" and "1984-1988" are dummy variables that take the value of 1 if the year falls within the specified range, 0 otherwise; the standard errors of the regression coefficients are in parentheses.

large, though falling short of the customary .05 significance level, for 1950–1988. But between 1950 and 1982 the trend was flat. Similarly, probit equations that take individual races as the unit of analysis reveal a substantial increase over time in the incumbent's probability of winning when the entire period is included, a smaller, though still significant increase when observations are restricted to 1950–1988, but no significant increase across the decades of the 1950s, 1960s, and 1970s. The same pattern appears when the proportion of winning incumbents is broken down by decade (Jacobson 1987a).

These data raise an important question: How could the unmistakable jump in the share of *votes* won by incumbents in the 1960s fail to raise their share of *victories* until the 1980s (when there was a further increase in their share of votes)? The answer lies in the larger electoral trend analyzed in Chapter 2: the growing volatility of House electorates, a component of the broader pattern of electoral disintegration.

A hypothetical example shows how greater variability in vote swings across districts could allow incumbents to win by wider average margins without becoming less vulnerable to defeat. Suppose the average incumbent wins with 55% of the vote and that the vote swing is normally distributed with a standard deviation of 5 percentage points. Other things equal, the average incumbent has about a .84 probability of winning the next election (see any table of areas under the normal curve). Now suppose the average incumbent's vote increases to 60%. If the standard deviation of the swing remains unchanged, the average incumbent's probability of reelection rises to .98. But if the standard deviation increases to 10 percentage points, the incumbent's seat is just as much at risk as before. Increasingly volatile electorates stretch the bounds of "marginality" if marginality is defined as a given risk of defeat.

Some evidence that the bounds of marginality have indeed widened are presented in Table 3.5. The 1970s—which include, by my definition, elections from 1972 through 1980—stand out in this regard. In the other decades, the average losing incumbent's margin in the previous election was about 55%; in the 1970s, it exceeded 58% (the median losing incumbent's vote was also 3 percentage points higher in the 1970s than in the other decades). While in the previous decades, only about 2% of the incumbents who had won with more than 60% of the two-party vote were defeated in the next election, 4.1% of these supposedly "nonmarginal" incumbents were defeated in the 1970s. More than 37% of the losing incumbents in the 1970s had won their previous election with more than 60% of the vote; in no other decade did this figure exceed 17%.

Monica Bauer and John Hibbing (1989) have argued that these differences are merely an artifact produced by the special circumstances of the 1974 election, in which some senior Republican members were punished for excessive loyalty to Richard Nixon. Certainly the 1974 results contribute strongly to the pattern; the mean 1972 vote share of Republicans who lost in 1974 had been 58.8%, and twelve of thirty-three had won more than 60% of the vote in 1972. But Bauer and Hibbing ignore the 1980 election in their discussion. The average 1978 vote for Democrats defeated in 1980 had been even higher—59.9%—and fourteen of the twenty-seven losers had won more than 60% of the vote in 1978, which had not been, it is important to emphasize, a good Democratic year (Republicans gained both seats and votes in the 1978 House elections).[6] The Democratic losses in 1980—including eight incumbents who had served nine or more terms, among them the majority whip and five committee chairmen—cannot be explained by individual or partisan scandal; they were the consequence of potent national political issues that could be turned to local advantage by Republican challengers.

In earlier decades, incumbents who had won the previous election handily were rarely among the defeated even in years when their party suffered very large losses. Comparative data are found in Table 3.6, which lists the percentage of losing incumbents who were ostensibly "nonmarginal" (having won more than 60% of the vote in the previous

TABLE 3.5
Widening Bounds of Marginality in House Elections, 1940s–1980s (in percentages)

Decade	Losing Incumbents' Mean Vote, $t-1$	Nonmarginal Incumbents Who Lost the Subsequent Election	Defeated Incumbents Who Were Nonmarginal
1940s	54.5	2.4	7.8
1950s	54.2	1.3	10.7
1960s	55.4	2.0	16.8
1970s	58.0	4.1	37.4
1980s	54.5	0.5	13.0

Note: Decades are defined by reapportionment cycles; for example, the 1950s include elections from 1952 through 1960; the 1940s include 1946–1950; the 1980s include 1982–1988. Nonmarginal incumbents are those who had won 60% or more of the two-party vote in the previous election.

TABLE 3.6
National Tides and Safety of House Incumbents, 1946–1980 (selected years)

Election Years with Major Swings	Incumbents Defeated	% Nonmarginal Year	Decade
1946	42	9.5	
1948	64	7.8	
1950	28	0.0	
1940s			6.7
1958	34	11.8	
1950s			11.8
1964	28	25.0	
1966	28	7.1	
1960s			16.1
1974	33	36.4	
1980	27	51.8	
1970s			43.3

Note: Election years with major swings are defined as those in which at least twenty-five incumbents were defeated; decades are defined by reapportionment cycles; nonmarginal incumbents are those who had won 60% or more of the two-party vote in the previous election.

TABLE 3.7
Vote Shift to House Challengers of Party Favored by National Swing, 1946–1988 (in percentages)

Decade	Vote Shift to Challengers Winners	Losers	Difference	Additional Vote Needed by Winning Challengers
1940s	8.7	4.2	4.5	−1.6
1950s	6.7	3.0	3.7	2.1
1960s	8.4	1.3	7.1	1.1
1970s	12.3	1.2	11.1	4.6
1980s	7.5	.8	6.3	3.2

Note: Decades are defined by reapportionment cycles; "additional vote needed by winning challengers" is the average percentage of votes that had to be added to the sum of (1) the vote for the candidate of the challenger's party in the previous election and (2) the national vote swing to the challenger's party for the total to reach 50.1%.

election) in election years in which their party's incumbents suffered aggregate losses of 25 or more seats. At the beginning of the period, even in years with very large swings against a party, very few of its losing incumbents had been "safe" by the 60% criterion. The proportion has increased each decade; in the last two elections in which more than twenty-five of a party's incumbents lost, 43.3% had been ostensibly "safe." Clearly, a wide margin of victory in one election is much weaker insurance against strongly contrary national tides than it once was.

Incumbents can still be defeated, but their individual fates are much less predictable from their previous vote margins and national swings. Table 3.7 presents two additional pieces of evidence to underline this point. The first three columns of the table compare the mean vote swings to winning and losing challengers representing the party gaining votes over the five decades. Note that, in recent decades, winning challengers have done much better than losing challengers—or than the national swing. The fourth column shows the percentage of votes winning challengers had to add to the sum of (1) the vote for their party's candidate last time and (2) the national vote swing to their party in order for their vote to reach 50.1%. The additional share of votes needed for victory is much higher in the two most recent decades than it was previously. Clearly, a successful challenge is far more dependent on the local effort than it once was.

In the 1940s and 1950s, incumbents who lost could blame forces largely beyond their control: district partisanship and national tides. No more. District electorates are no longer reliably partisan; national tides may still help to defeat incumbents, but not without considerable local augmentation. And that depends on the quality and vigor of the opposition, which are the subjects of the next chapter.

NOTES

1. Recent examples include Jacobson (1987b); Alford and Brady (1988); Ansolabehere, Brady, and Fiorina (1988); Bauer and Hibbing (1989); and Gelman and King (1989).

2. The regression equation is

$$\text{incumbents' vote share (\%)} = \underset{(.37)}{58.87} + \underset{(.03)}{.41} \times \text{election year}$$

Adjusted R^2 = .91, Durbin-Watson = 1.55, number of cases = 22

3. I have included redrawn districts (and election years ending in 2) in this part of the analysis for the simple reason that the patterns are identical with or without them.

4. The regression equation is

$$\text{partisan advantage (\%)} = \underset{(1.18)}{59.01} - \underset{(.09)}{.12} \times \text{election year}$$

Adjusted R^2 = .03, Durbin-Watson = 1.69, number of cases = 22

5. At least part of this anomaly can be traced to some peculiarities of the 1964 and 1966 elections in the South. Though swamped elsewhere, Republicans gained seats in the deep South in 1964. Three of the Republican victors sought higher office rather than reelection in 1966, and their seats swung back to Democrats with an average shift of -21.6 percentage points despite the strong national tide favoring Republicans elsewhere. This contributed to the remarkable 16.9-point difference in the vote swing between Republican districts held by incumbents ($+9.7$ points) and left open by retirement (-7.2 points), and hence to the large measured increase in the incumbency advantage, in 1966. The difference in the mean swing for seats held by Democrats was a much more modest 4.9 points.

6. These analyses include only those incumbents who were not freshmen and whose districts were not redrawn between the first and second election.

4

You Can't Beat Somebody with Nobody: Trends in Partisan Opposition

In the previous chapter, we observed that by several standards—not least by the crucial standard of winning reelection—the electoral value of House incumbency reached a new plateau in the 1984–1988 period. The 1988 election was particularly striking in this respect: Despite George Bush's decisive victory in the presidential contest, incumbent Democrats as well as Republicans actually improved on their 1986 vote. A curious thing about this change is that it was not associated with any of the other trends that have been offered as explanations for the earlier expansion of the incumbency advantage. It was not connected with a further decrease in party loyalty, because party loyalty actually increased a bit during the period (see Figure 2.3). It is not associated with any growth in ticket splitting or divided outcomes, because partisan consistency edged upward in all the figures during this period (Figures 2.4, 2.6, and 2.7). Nor can it be attributed to further growth in congressional office and staff resources, because growth in perks flattened out in the 1980s under the pressure of tight budgets and, perhaps, natural saturation (Ornstein, Mann, and Malbin 1990:132, 134, 144–145).

I shall argue in this chapter that the explanation is not to be found in the behavior of incumbents or voters, but in the quality and vigor of challenges to incumbents. House incumbents did unusually well in these elections because their opposition was unusually feeble. House Republicans took little advantage of their 1984 and 1988 presidential victories because they did not field enough challengers capable of exploiting favorable partisan trends. The strength of the challenges is endogenous, of course, so the explanation cannot stop here. But it is an essential starting point. To understand what has happened, we need to examine changes over the past forty years in both the intensity and electoral importance of local opposition to incumbents. Trends in opposition go far to explain why recent House elections have produced so few incumbent defeats, and they also help to account for the Republicans' failure to make gains in the House during the 1980s.

UNOPPOSED CANDIDATES

The initial requirement for competitive elections is that both parties field candidates.[1] Incumbents are certainly secure if no one chooses to challenge them; a party cannot lose an open seat if the other party does not field a candidate. The incidence of unopposed candidacies has undergone at least two significant changes during the postwar period. These changes are the subject of this section.

The broad pattern of change over time in uncontested seats is revealed in Figure 4.1, which shows how the proportion of unopposed incumbents and uncontested open seats has varied in elections from 1946 through 1988. Few open seats are ignored by either party; since 1954, no election year has produced more than 2 uncontested open seats. A much higher proportion of incumbents go unopposed, and two clear trends appear in the data. The first is a precipitous drop in the proportion of unopposed incumbents between 1958 and 1964; the 1964 election featured the smallest number (forty-three) and proportion (11%) of unopposed incumbents in any postwar congressional election. After 1964, this trend reversed; the incidence of unopposed incumbents rebounded to the point where, in 1988, the number (seventy-nine) and proportion (19.4%) of incumbents given a free ride reached levels not approached since the 1950s.

The sharp drop in unopposed incumbents through 1964 has a ready explanation. It signals the rapid emergence of two-party competition in parts of the South where Republicans had not run candidates since Reconstruction.[2] In retrospect, the 1964 election was a decisive moment in the breakup of the New Deal coalition; Barry Goldwater's conspicuous opposition to the Civil Rights Act of 1964 accelerated the movement of Southern politicians as well as voters into the Republican party. With the spread of Republican candidacies across the South, neither party enjoyed unchallenged dominance in any region.

The South's contribution to increased House competition in the early 1960s is clear from Figure 4.2, which tracks the number of unopposed incumbents within and outside the South since 1946. Figure 4.2 also shows that, despite more frequent opposition, Southern incumbents are still considerably more likely to run unopposed and that competition for Southern House seats has, by this measure, changed little since 1964. The growth in uncontested seats since 1964 has occurred in regions outside the South. By 1988, major-party challengers were absent in almost as many districts outside the South as in it, although unopposed

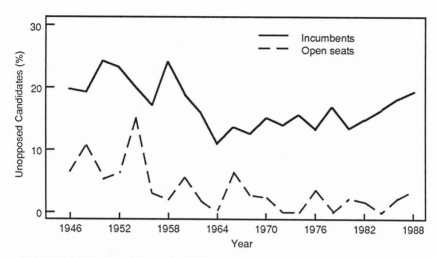

FIGURE 4.1 Unopposed House Candidates, 1946–1988

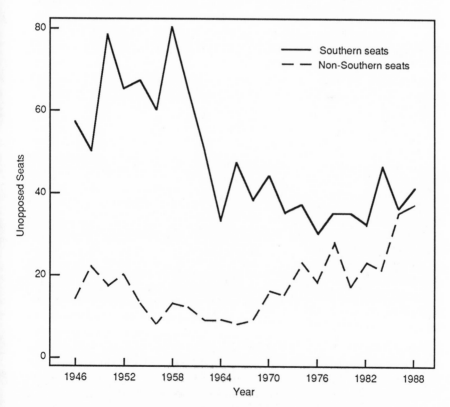

FIGURE 4.2 Uncontested Southern and non-Southern House Seats, 1946–1988

incumbents are still a good deal more common in Southern districts, because the region holds only about one-fourth of all House seats.

The emergence of two-party competition in the South inevitably had partisan repercussions, because the Democrats initially held almost every uncontested Southern House seat. Through 1964, more competition meant more challenges to Democratic incumbents. After 1964, the number of uncontested incumbents of both parties drifted irregularly upward, as Figure 4.3 demonstrates. Democrats still maintain a substantial advantage in free rides, but Republicans have narrowed the gap considerably since the 1950s.

Again, however, strong regional differences emerge. Through 1964, few (11%) uncontested Republican seats were located in the South; since then, a majority of them (57%) have been located there. By winning seats in the South, Republicans have inherited some of the benefit of the region's propensity to leave incumbents alone. Outside the South, however, Democratic incumbents have reaped the lion's share of the growing number of uncontested seats. Figure 4.4 presents the evidence (in raw seats—percentages would make the same general point, but seats tell the politically more important story). As we shall see, this is but one sign of the Republican party's growing weakness in House elections outside the South.

Measured by the presence of candidates from both major parties, competition for House seats expanded sharply in the early 1960s, then subsequently atrophied. How do these changes relate to other measures of competition? Intuitively, the average vote for challengers ought to decline when challengers begin to appear in large numbers in districts once monopolized by the incumbent's party. Because initial challengers win a smaller share of the vote than average—the mean vote for challengers in districts where the incumbent was unopposed in the previous election is less than 30% for the postwar period—expanded opposition ought to be associated with a decrease in the average challenger's vote.

Through 1964, this was indeed the pattern. Since then, however, the challenger's share of the vote in contested elections has continued to decline, while the proportion of unopposed incumbents has grown. The 1988 election occasioned a low point in the first trend and a high point in the second. Not only were there proportionately fewer major-party challenges than at any time in thirty years, the share of votes won by the challengers who did run was among the lowest on record. This brings us back to the question posed at the beginning of this chapter: Why have challenges seemed so futile in recent House elections? The answer requires a look at challengers.

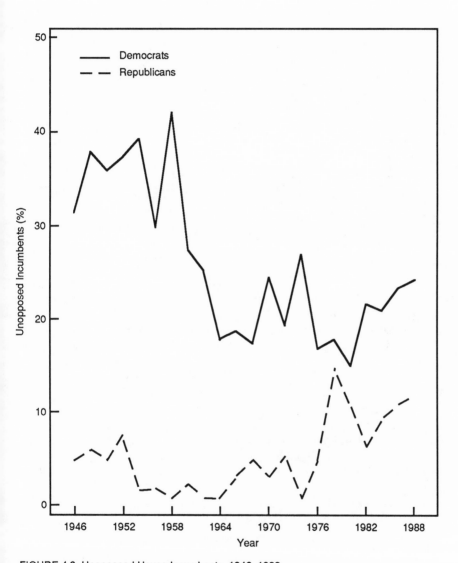

FIGURE 4.3 Unopposed House Incumbents, 1946–1988

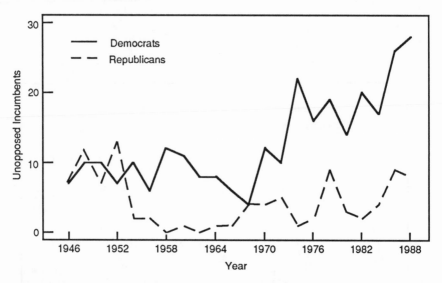

FIGURE 4.4 Unopposed Non-Southern Incumbents, 1946–1988

THE CHALLENGERS

Insofar as House elections are candidate rather than party centered, competition depends on the political talents and resources, not merely the presence, of challengers. To the degree that voters' decisions are shaped by their responses to the choice offered between a particular pair of candidates at the district level, the individual characteristics of the candidates, the extent and content of their campaigns, are crucial. With few exceptions, House incumbents are accomplished campaigners with adequate resources to conduct full-scale campaigns. Usually their challengers are not. Under all but the most unusual circumstances, only attractive, well-funded challengers pose a serious electoral threat to incumbents (Jacobson 1987b). The growth of candidate-centered electoral politics has thus enhanced the importance of the challenger during the postwar period.

To demonstrate that the quality of the challenger makes a difference, and that the difference quality makes has grown over the past four decades, a measure of quality is required. For this analysis, I resort to a simple dichotomy: whether or not the candidate has ever held elective public office of any kind. Candidates who have held elective office are considered high-quality, experienced candidates; the others are not. Notice that by this standard, all House incumbents are, by definition, high-quality candidates. More elaborate and nuanced measures of candidate quality have been developed, but I stick with this simple dichotomy

TABLE 4.1
Political Experience and Frequency of Victory in House Elections, 1946–1988

Type of Race	Number of Cases	Winners (%)*
Open seats		
Incumbent party candidate experienced	361	87.0
Neither candidate experienced	194	76.8
Both candidates experienced	206	66.5
Challenging party candidate experienced	101	50.4
Challengers to incumbents		
Candidate experienced	1,769	17.3
Candidate not experienced	5,334	4.3

*For open seats, percentage of victories for party currently holding the seat.

because it is objective, noncircular, and, most crucially, available for the entire postwar period.[3]

If quality matters, and if experience in elective office indicates quality, then, at minimum, experienced candidates ought to win more victories than inexperienced candidates. Table 4.1 shows that they do. Candidates who have held elective office are much more likely to win. Experienced challengers are four times as likely as inexperienced challengers to defeat incumbents. Candidates for open seats with prior experience in elective office are also more likely to win, their chances depending also on whether their opponents are similarly experienced (as well as on which party already held the seat). For (new) open seats held by neither party, experienced candidates win four of five contests against candidates who have never held elective office (N = 59, data not shown).

Of course, if high-quality challengers follow rational career strategies, they do not appear randomly. Other things equal, the better the odds on winning, the more likely they are to run. Ambitious, experienced career politicians make the most formidable candidates for Congress because they have the greatest incentive and opportunity to cultivate the political skills and connections that lead to effective candidacies. They also risk the most in trying to move to higher office, for defeat may retard or end their career. Thus the best potential candidates are also the most sensitive to the odds on winning and so to conditions that affect the odds.

One major consideration is the availability of money and other campaign resources. Astute career politicians do not enter contests without some reasonable expectation that they can assemble the wherewithal to mount a full-scale campaign. People who control campaign resources also deploy them strategically. They do not invest in hopeless causes; more favorable prospects inspire more generous support. Among the things they consider is the quality of the candidate. Better candidates attract more resources, just as the availability of resources attracts better candidates (Jacobson 1980; Jacobson and Kernell 1983).

A simple demonstration that high-quality candidates make strategic career decisions based on the prospects for advancement is presented in Table 4.2. Open seats attract the largest share of experienced candidates, but within this category, it makes a great deal of difference which party holds the seat because this has such a large effect on the chances of winning. Candidates for open seats who are unopposed always win, of course, and high-quality candidates are most common in these races. Among challengers, the incumbent's margin of victory in the previous election is strongly related to the proportions of both victories and high-quality challengers.

Clearly, career politicians are acutely sensitive to local conditions that affect electoral odds.[4] They are also sensitive to national conditions— the state of the economy, the performance of the administration, scandals, and crises—that promise to help or hinder candidates of their party, though, as we shall see, Democrats are far more responsive to national conditions than are Republicans (Jacobson and Kernell 1983; Jacobson 1989). Electoral expectations, then, have a powerful effect on candidacies: The better the prospects, the better the challengers and the more resources they have for their campaigns; the bleaker the outlook, the more feeble the challenge. Thus we would expect an inverse relationship between the strength of a challenge and the incumbent's electoral performance even if the strength of the challenge had no independent effect on the outcome.

In fact, however, the strength of the challenge has, by itself, a major impact on election results. The success enjoyed by high-quality candidates is not merely a consequence of more careful selection of targets, though such strategic behavior certainly contributes to it. Higher quality candidates run when the chances of winning are better, but they contribute independently to the outcome. Much of the evidence for this conclusion is available elsewhere (Jacobson and Kernell 1983; Jacobson 1989), but I shall summarize the key results here, because understanding this connection is central to understanding changes in postwar electoral competition.

The equations in Table 4.3 show that experienced candidates win a larger share of the votes and enjoy a higher probability of winning, even when local and national political circumstances are taken into account. The table reports results from two models. The first regresses the challenger's percentage of the vote on a constant and three variables: the vote for the candidate of the challenger's party in the previous election (a measure of the incumbent's local vulnerability), the national two-party vote shift for the challenger's party in the election year (a

TABLE 4.2
Probability of Victory and Quality of Nonincumbent Candidates for the House, 1946–1988

Type of Race	Number of Cases	Winners (%)	Former Officeholders (%)
Open seats			
No general election opponent	34	100.0	82.4
Held by candidate's party	862	79.7	65.7
Held by neither party	194	50.0	52.1
Held by opposite party	862	20.3	35.6
Challengers to incumbents			
Incumbent's vote in last election (%)			
50.0–54.9	1,546	20.2	45.3
55.0–59.9	1,467	8.6	28.9
60.0–64.9	1,338	3.8	19.7
65.0–69.9	1,124	2.3	14.6
70.0 or more	1,670	0.6	8.9

TABLE 4.3
Elective Office Experience and Challenger's Success in House Elections, 1946–1988 and 1972–1988

Variable	Regression		Probit	
	1946–1988 (1)	1972–1988 (2)	1946–1988 (3)	1972–1988 (4)
Intercept	9.87***	9.19***	−5.65***	−5.53***
	(.34)	(.76)	(.23)	(.50)
Vote of challenger's party in last election (%)	.70***	.34***	.09***	.03***
	(.01)	(.01)	(.01)	(.01)
National shift in two-party vote (%)	.95***	.69***	.18***	.14***
	(.02)	(.03)	(.01)	(.02)
Challenger is experienced	2.77***	1.56***	.44***	.29**
	(.19)	(.27)	(.06)	(.11)
Challenger's spending (log $1,000s)		3.73***		.95***
		(.10)		(.09)
Incumbent's spending (log $1,000s)		−.48**		−.45***
		(.16)		(.10)
Adjusted R^2	.58	.68		
Log likelihood			−1,219	−363
Number of cases	6,453	2,667	6,453	2,667

**p < .01, one-tailed test.
***p < .001, one-tailed test.

Note: The dependent variable for the regression equations in columns 1 and 2 is the challenger's percentage of the two-party vote; its coefficients are regression coefficients. The dependent variable for the probit equations in columns 3 and 4 is 1 if the challenger won, 0 otherwise; its coefficients are maximum likelihood estimates. The national shift in the two-party vote is the change in the percentage of votes won nationally by the challenger's party in the election. Experienced challengers are those who have previously held elective offices (scored 1, otherwise, 0). Spending is entered as the log of spending in $1,000s, with a minimum of $5,000 assumed for each candidate. Standard errors are in parentheses.

measure of national trends), and whether or not the challenger has held elective office. In the second model, the independent variables are the same, but the dependent variable is categorical (whether the challenger won or not), so the coefficients are estimated by probit rather than regression.

The results indicate that experience has a significant impact on votes and victories controlling for the kind of local and national political conditions that would affect career strategies. According to the regression coefficient, other things equal, a high-quality candidate was worth an additional 2.8% of the vote. The probit coefficient cannot be interpreted so directly, because its effect depends on the probability of victory established by the other variables. The appropriate computation shows that conditions giving an inexperienced challenger a .05 probability of victory would give a high-quality candidate a .11 probability of victory; in the same fashion .10 would grow to .20, .20 to .34, for a high-quality compared to a low-quality challenger.

Table 4.3 also reports equations covering the 1972–1988 period that include as independent variables campaign spending by the challenger and the incumbent (usable campaign spending data have been available only since 1972). Because diminishing returns applies to campaign spending, the expenditure variables are entered as the natural log of spending in $1,000s.[5]

The inclusion of campaign spending reduces the coefficient on quality, as theory would suggest. Because contributors also act strategically, quality and campaign spending are positively correlated; experienced challengers, on average, spend more than twice as much as inexperienced challengers. But even controlling for spending, experienced challengers do significantly better than inexperienced challengers in winning votes and victories. Clearly, both money and quality contribute to the strength of a challenge.

Notice also that the marginal returns on spending are much larger for challengers than for incumbents. This is not at all surprising (Jacobson 1980, 1985, 1990a); the surprise is finding that spending by incumbents has *any* significant effect on the vote share or probability of winning in a model of this sort. When analyses are confined to single election years, as has been customary in studies of campaign spending effects, none of the coefficients on incumbent spending in either equation achieves significance ($p < .05$), and incorrect signs are not uncommon (Jacobson 1985b). Results of this sort have been puzzling: If spending by House incumbents really had no effect, why would they put so much effort into raising funds, and why would they invariably spend more money the more seriously they were challenged? In an earlier paper, I speculated that

[o]ne possible explanation is that spending by incumbents provides tiny but positive marginal returns, so that it makes perfect sense for incumbents to spend large amounts of money to counteract serious challenges. After all, when an incumbent is defeated, it is normally in a close contest; small shifts in the vote make the difference between victory and defeat. Even if the . . . effects of spending [on votes] are too small to be measured amid the noise in the data, they may be large enough to be worth the effort (1985b:41).

The results of equations 2 and 4 in Table 4.3 are consistent with this view. The large number of observations produced by combining all nine election years mitigates the problem of noisy data, and a more precise estimate of how spending by incumbents affects the vote emerges in equation 2. The marginal return in votes on campaign expenditures is still almost eight times greater for challengers, but spending by incumbents does have a significant payoff in votes as well. The coefficient in equation 4 indicates that spending by incumbents has a relatively stronger effect on the electoral bottom line—winning or losing—though the impact of spending by challengers remains considerably larger. By this evidence, it is not at all irrational for incumbents to spend large sums in response to vigorous challenges. Despite the fact that, in simple terms, the more incumbents spend, the worse they do on election day (the simple correlation between the incumbent's level of expenditures and share of votes or probability of victory are −.38 and −.14, respectively), reactive spending can partially offset the challenger's gains from more vigorous campaigning.

THE GROWING IMPACT OF THE CHALLENGER

By the logic of the arguments advanced in this book, the impact of the challenger's personal quality should have grown as electoral politics became more candidate-centered over the postwar period. In an earlier era of stronger party attachments and longer presidential coattails, local outcomes were more subject to district partisanship and national political tides. Strategic decisions were at least as critical to successful electoral careers, but the personal quality of individual candidates was of smaller electoral consequence. Over time, the emergence of a more candidate-centered style of electoral politics reduced the electoral importance of partisan forces while enhancing that of specific candidates and campaigns. Thus the resources and talents of challengers should have an increasing impact on district-level results.

Evidence that the expected change did occur is found in Table 4.4. The table presents a regression model equivalent to equation 1 and a

TABLE 4.4

Growing Impact of Quality of Challengers in House Elections, 1946–1988

Variable	Regression (1)	Probit (2)
Intercept	8.37***	−7.96***
	(.78)	(.50)
Vote of challenger's party in last election (%)	.80***	.15***
	(.02)	(.01)
National shift in two-party vote (%)	.94***	.18***
	(.02)	(.01)
Experienced challenger	1.17**	.44***
	(.38)	(.11)
Election year	.18***	.19***
	(.05)	(.03)
Election year × vote of challengers's party in last election (%)	−.011***	−.005***
	(.001)	(.001)
Election year × experienced challenger	.14***	−.001
	(.03)	(.009)
Adjusted R^2	.60	
Log likelihood		−1,198
Number of cases	6,453	6,453

**p < .01, one-tailed test.

***p < .001, one-tailed test.

Note: The dependent variable for the regression equation in column 1 is the challenger's percentage of the two-party vote; its coefficients are regression coefficients. The dependent variable for the probit equation in column 2 is 1 if the challenger won, 0 otherwise; its coefficients are maximum likelihood estimates. The national shift in the two-party vote is the change in the percentage of votes won nationally by the challenger's party in the election. Experienced challengers are those who have previously held elective offices (scored 1, otherwise, 0). The values of "election year" are 1946 = 1, 1948 = 2, . . . 1988 = 22. Standard errors are in parentheses.

probit model equivalent to equation 2 in Table 4.3, but with the addition of a trend term (1946 = 1, 1948 = 2, . . . , 1988 = 22) and interactions between the trend term and the vote of the challenger's party in the previous election and the challenger's quality.

The first equation in Table 4.4 indicates that the payoff for quality in terms of votes increased significantly between 1946 and 1988. According to the regression coefficients, its value grew from 1.2 percentage points in 1946 to 4.3 percentage points in 1988. At the same time, consistent with the evidence of dissociation examined in Chapter 2, continuity between elections has diminished significantly; the impact of the prior vote fell from .78 to .57.[6] Prior results also have a smaller impact than they once did on the challenger's prospects of victory (equation 2 in

Table 4.4), but the impact of quality on victory has not changed at all. Evidently, a high-quality challenge made as large a contribution to the probability of victory forty years ago as it does now.

Although the regression and probit findings might appear at odds with one another, they make sense in light of the postwar electoral trends we have discussed. In the 1940s and 1950s, contests between challengers and incumbents were typically closer than they are today; electorates were more loyally partisan, and district vote swings tracked national vote swings more faithfully. The presence of a high-quality challenger may have had a smaller direct effect on the vote, but in the more competitive electoral environment, it was sufficient to raise the probability of victory substantially. Since the 1950s, electoral competition between House incumbents and challengers, as measured by vote margins, has diminished. The increment in votes enjoyed by experienced challengers has grown, but the distance challengers must make up to overtake the incumbent has grown even more.

Measured in votes, the increased value of a high-quality challenge almost matched the increased value of incumbency from the 1950s to the 1970s. This helps to explain why, despite wider average vote margins, House seats did not become significantly more secure over these decades (recall Chapter 3). But it indicates that a successful challenge is now far more contingent on local circumstances—on particular candidates and campaigns—than it once was.

CHANGES IN THE QUALITY OF CHALLENGERS

The quality of candidates and campaigns has a major effect on House election results, and the effect has, in some respects, grown over the past forty years. How has the quality of candidates changed over the postwar period? And how have these changes affected competition for House seats?

Although the importance of a strong challenge has increased over the postwar period, the incidence of strong challenges changed little— until very recently. Figure 4.5 displays the percentage of experienced challengers taking on incumbents in elections from 1946 through 1988. The lower line includes all incumbent-held seats in the denominator; the upper line presents the proportion of high-quality candidates among all major-party challengers that did appear. The two measures of aggregate quality track each other closely.

There is no sign of a trend other than the notable drop in the aggregate quality of House challengers in the late 1980s. Again the 1988 elections stand out: Not only was the number of unopposed incumbents the highest in thirty years, the proportion of high-quality candidates among all major-party challengers who did run was only 12.3%, more than two standard deviations below the 1946–1986 mean of 21.3%.

Another key difference between the 1984–1988 election period and earlier periods is that *both* parties fielded relatively weak challengers. This is unexpected, because strategic considerations should normally lead the parties' potential candidates to opposite decisions. When national conditions—the economy, popular ratings of the president's performance—favor a party, more of its experienced, high-quality candidates should run, because the chances of winning are assumed to be better. The other party's experienced candidates should be more inclined to wait for a more propitious year. And, indeed, the *relative* aggregate quality of a party's challengers has been strongly related to national conditions over the postwar period (Jacobson 1989). But most of this has been the Democrats' doing; Republican challengers have been consistently less sensitive to national conditions than have their Democratic counterparts, and they have been particularly insensitive in recent elections.

Two types of evidence establish these points. Table 4.5 presents probit equations estimating the probability that an experienced challenger opposed the incumbent, given local and national conditions. Local opportunities expected to influence career moves are measured by the percentage of votes won by the candidate of the challenger's party, and whether the seat switched party hands, in the previous election. The economy and the president's level of popular approval measure the national conditions. A fifth variable, the party of the administration (scored 1 if Democratic, 0 if Republican) must be entered as a control because of the way some of the other variables are scored.

The state of the economy is measured as the percentage change in real disposable income per capita over the year ending in the second quarter of the election year.[7] Because the administration's party (not just the Democratic party) is supposed to be rewarded or punished for its management of the economy, this variable is multiplied by -1 when a Republican is in the White House (this is why the administration dummy is required). Presidential approval is scored as the mean percentage of citizens approving of the president's performance in Gallup Polls taken during the second quarter of the election year.[8] Again, this variable is multiplied by -1 under Republican administrations. National conditions are measured in the second quarter (April–June) of the election year because this is the period during which most *final* decisions about candidacy must be made.[9]

Finally, a party should field experienced challengers more frequently when it has a larger pool of experienced candidates from which to draw. We would not, for example, expect to find many experienced Republican

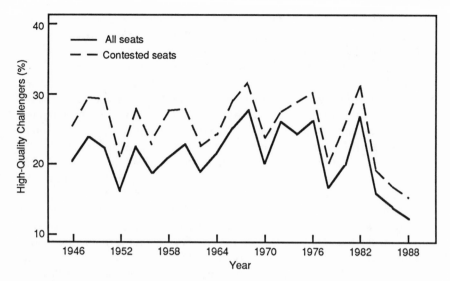

FIGURE 4.5 Quality of House Challengers, 1946–1988

TABLE 4.5
Estimates of Probability that House Challenger Has Held Elective Office, 1946–1988

Variable	Democrats (1)	Republicans (2)
Intercept	−2.25***	.70**
	(.19)	(.25)
Party of administration	−.79***	.49*
	(.20)	(.22)
Change in party control of seat last election	.51***	.53***
	(.08)	(.08)
Votes won by Democratic candidate in last election (%)	.038***	−.037***
	(.004)	(.003)
Change in real income per capita (2nd quarter)	.047***	−.012
	(.010)	(.010)
Presidential approval (2nd quarter)	.005*	−.003
	(.002)	(.002)
Candidate pool	.235***	.301***
	(.031)	(.035)
Log likelihood	−1,718	−1,618
Number of cases	3,349	3,729

*p < .05, one-tailed test.
**p < .01, one-tailed test.
***p < .001, one-tailed test.

Note: See text for a description of the variables; standard errors are in parentheses.

challengers in the South prior to the mid-1960s because Republicans held so few elective offices in the region. For convenience (the data are readily available) and because by far the most common stepping-stone to Congress is the state legislature, I estimate the size of the pool as the ratio of the total number of seats a party holds in the state legislature at the time of the election to the number of House seats in the state. The distribution of this ratio is highly skewed—New Hampshire, for example, currently has 524 state legislators squeezed into its two House districts—so this variable is entered as its natural logarithm.[10]

The first equation in Table 4.5 indicates that all of the local and national conditions significantly affect the probability that a high-quality Democratic candidate challenged the Republican incumbent. All of the coefficients have the appropriate sign and are more than twice their standard errors. Republican challengers, in contrast, appear to be sensitive only to local circumstances, though the coefficients on the items measuring national conditions show the correct signs, and presidential approval does not fall too far short of conventional levels of statistical significance.

Aggregate data tell a similar story. In Table 4.6, the dependent variables are the percentages of Democratic and Republican challengers who have held elective office, and the difference between these two percentages, in postwar House elections. They are regressed on the economic and presidential approval variables, plus the current partisan division of House seats. This last variable serves double duty in these equations. It acknowledges that the more seats a party holds, the greater the number of inviting targets it presents to the opposing party regardless of other circumstances (Oppenheimer, Stimson, and Waterman 1986). But it also serves as a more general measure of opportunity: Substantial gains by a party in one election are commonly followed by substantial losses in the next (a majority of which do *not* consist of seats captured from the other party in the previous election; recall Table 2.3), and strategic politicians should take this cycle of "surge and decline" (Campbell 1960) into account. As before, the scoring of the other independent variables makes it necessary to control for the party of the administration.

Again, economic conditions and the level of public approval of the president have a significant and substantial impact on the quality of Democratic challengers. Neither one matters for Republicans, who are sensitive only to the opportunities offered by the current level of Democratic strength in the House. However, a composite variable measuring the relative quality of challengers is affected significantly by all of these variables. This is the key variable, because relative quality is what matters on election day (Jacobson 1989).

By these measures, Democratic challengers are, individually and in aggregate, clearly more "strategic" than Republican challengers. The

TABLE 4.6
Determinants of Percentage of Experienced House Challengers, 1946–1988

Variable	Democrats (1)	Republicans (2)	Democrats − Republicans (3)
Intercept	53.05*** (12.74)	−11.44 (11.68)	64.49*** (14.01)
Party of administration	−27.67** (8.90)	12.28 (8.15)	−39.95*** (9.79)
Seats won by Democrats last election (%)	−.22 (.19)	.36* (.17)	−.58** (.21)
Change in real income per capita (2nd quarter)	1.44** (.44)	.23 (.40)	1.20** (.49)
Presidential approval (2nd quarter)	.20* (.09)	−.11 (.08)	.31** (.10)
Adjusted R^2	.52	.12	.60
Durbin-Watson	1.23	1.59	1.56
Number of cases	22	22	22

*p < .05, one-tailed test.
**p < .01, one-tailed test.
***p < .001, one-tailed test.

Note: The dependent variable in equations 1 and 2 is the percentage of challengers of the designated party who have held elective office; for equation 2, the dependent variable is the difference between the two; the independent variables are described in the text; standard errors are in parentheses.

difference is even more pronounced when analysis is confined to the 1966–1988 period. *None* of the coefficients is significant (t-ratios all below 1.0) when equation 2 in Table 4.6 is reestimated for elections since 1966. The probit coefficients representing national conditions in equations like those in Table 4.5 also have larger standard errors (and income shows the wrong sign) when analysis covers only the past two decades. Thus the quality of Republican challengers has not varied systematically with the party's national electoral prospects, particularly during the recent period of Republican presidential ascendancy. But the quality of Republican challengers has just as strong an impact on election results as does the quality of Democratic challengers. The coefficients on terms interacting party and quality in alternative versions of the equations in Table 4.3 are substantively small and statistically insignificant for the 1968–1988 period; analysis of aggregate data sustains the same point (Jacobson 1989:784). One reason for the Republican party's inability to advance in the House thus may be its failure to field candidates of sufficient quality to take full advantage of favorable conditions. Let us investigate further.

FIGURE 4.6 Quality of Democratic and Republican House Challengers, 1946–1988

PARTISAN TRENDS IN THE QUALITY
OF CHALLENGERS

Throughout the postwar period, Republicans have, in every year save 1966, fielded proportionately fewer experienced challengers than have Democrats, as Figure 4.6 demonstrates. The average difference is substantial: For the entire period, 27.0% of Republican incumbents faced high-quality challengers, compared to only 16.5% of the Democratic incumbents. And although no general trend in the incidence of experienced challengers over the entire postwar era is evident for either party (regression slopes for the data points connected in Figure 4.6 are not significantly different from zero), there is some evidence that the Republican party has found it increasingly difficult to recruit experienced challengers during the last two decades. Table 4.7 shows the results of regressing the percentage of Democratic incumbents facing experienced Republican challengers on time (1966 = 1, 1968 = 2, . . . 1988 = 12), and whether the election is a midterm election, from 1966 through 1988. The coefficients indicate that the Democratic incumbents have faced increasingly weak Republican challenges (by the criterion of experience) during the period of Republican presidential dominance, though high-quality Republican challenges are significantly more common in presidential election years.

The falloff of experienced Republican challengers has been especially noticeable in districts outside the South. The dramatic growth in the number of Republicans challenging Southern Democrats in the early 1960s was accompanied by a sharp increase in the number of high-quality Republican House candidates in the region; the party went from fielding virtually no experienced challengers in the 1940s and 1950s to fielding an average of 9.0% in the 1960s. But since that time, the average quality of Republican House challengers in the South has changed very little; it was no higher in the 1980s (8.8% with experience) than in the 1960s. Meanwhile, however, the quality of Republican challengers outside the South has declined. Republicans are less than half as likely as they were forty years ago to field an experienced challenger against a Democratic incumbent outside the South. Their average for the 1946–1950 period was 29.3%; for 1984–1988 it was 13.0%. While the party became more competitive in the South, it became less competitive elsewhere in terms of the quality of its challengers as well as by the measure of running any candidate at all.[11]

THE COLLAPSE OF COMPETITION, 1984–1988

The growth of the incumbency advantage through the early 1980s cannot be attributed to any systematic decline in the aggregate quality of House challengers, because the aggregate quality of challengers did not decline. Since 1984, however, extraordinarily weak challenges have coincided with a notable increase in the electoral performance of incumbents.

The aggregate weakness of challengers in these elections is indicated by measures beyond the simple index of experience in elective office. For example, Donald Green and Jonathan Krasno have developed an elaborate nine-point scale measuring challenger quality in elections from 1972 through 1986; challengers had the lowest mean quality score on this scale in 1986, the second lowest in 1984 (Krasno and Green 1988; Green 1989). In real dollars, the average challenger's campaign spending declined in each successive election after 1982, while expenditures by

64

TABLE 4.7
Decline in Quality of Republican Challengers, 1966–1988

Variable	(1)
Intercept	27.63***
	(2.37)
Midterm election	−4.43*
	(1.92)
Election year	−1.27***
	(.28)
Adjusted R^2	.66
Durbin-Watson	1.97
Number of cases	12

*p < .05, one-tailed test.
***p < .001, one-tailed test.

Note: The dependent variable is the percentage of Republican challengers who had held elective office; "midterm election" takes the value of 1 for midterm election years, 0 for presidential election years; the values of "election year" are 1966 = 1, 1968 = 2, . . . 1988 = 12; standard errors are in parentheses.

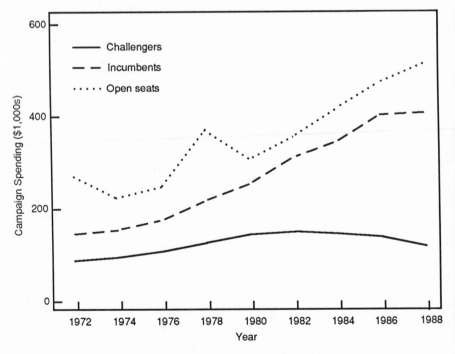

FIGURE 4.7 Campaign Spending in House Elections, 1972–1988

incumbents and candidates for open seats continued to rise steeply. Figure 4.7 displays the relevant data. The average challenger spent less money on the campaign in 1988 than in any election since 1976; fewer challengers spent beyond $300,000—a conservative threshold for a serious challenge (Jacobson 1987c)—in 1988 than in any election since 1978.

Republican challenges were especially feeble in 1988. Measured by experience, the quality of Republican challengers reached a postwar low; the average Republican challenger spent less money, and fewer Republican challengers exceeded the $300,000 threshold for an adequately funded campaign, than in any election since 1974. Over the entire twenty-year period of Republican presidential ascendancy, only in 1974, the worst Republican year in two decades, did Republicans mount weaker challenges than in 1988. No wonder George Bush's victory failed to increase Republican representation in the House.

The aggregate weakness of Republican challenges is a genuine puzzle. The boost given to the party's long-term prospects by growing Republican partisanship in the electorate (see Chapter 6) and a succession of presidential victories should, one would think, encourage challengers to take on Democratic incumbents and spur Republican donors to finance their campaigns. Why have Republicans not fielded more experienced, well-funded challengers in recent years? We do not know yet; I shall examine some possible explanations in the final chapter.

QUALITY CANDIDATES IN OPEN SEATS

The data in Table 4.1 suggest that the quality of candidates also makes an important difference in contests for open seats. Candidates for open seats who have held elective office win more frequently, with their chances depending also on whether their opponents are high-quality candidates. This relationship survives when the appropriate controls are imposed, and, as the equations in Table 4.8 reveal, the quality of the candidate representing the party *not* currently holding the seat makes the most difference.

The first equation in Table 4.8 displays the results of regressing the share of votes won by the candidate of the party currently holding an open seat on its vote in the previous election, the national two-party vote swing, and the quality of the two candidates. Notice that the coefficient on the quality of the out-party's candidate is almost five times as large as that on the quality of the in-party's candidate. The second equation repeats the analysis taking the in-party's victory or defeat as the dependent variable and using probit to estimate the parameters. The quality of both candidates has a substantively large and statistically significant impact on the outcome. Again, the quality of the out-party's

TABLE 4.8
Impact of Quality of Challengers in House Elections for Open Seats, 1946–1988

Variable	Regression (1)	Probit (2)
Intercept	24.58***	−1.65***
	(2.34)	(.43)
Winner's vote in last election (%)	.54***	.039***
	(.04)	(.007)
National shift in two-party vote (%)	.70***	.106***
	(.08)	(.015)
Experienced challenger, in-party	1.25*	.39***
	(.70)	(.12)
Experienced challenger, out-party	−6.11***	−.74***
	(.68)	(.11)
Adjusted R²	.37	
Log likelihood		−329
Number of cases	694	694

*p < .05, one-tailed test.
***p < .001, one-tailed test.

Note: The dependent variable for the regression equation (1) is the percentage of the two-party vote won by the candidate of the party currently holding the open seat; its coefficients are regression coefficients. The dependent variable for the probit equation (2) is 1 if the in-party's candidate won, 0 otherwise; its coefficients are maximum likelihood estimates. "National shift in two-party vote" is the change in the percentage of votes won nationally by in-party from the last election. Experienced challengers are those who have previously held elective offices (scored 1, otherwise, 0). Standard errors are in parentheses.

candidate makes the larger difference in the results. In contests for open seats, the coefficients on candidate quality do not change over time (the interaction terms are insignificant), but there is a similar decrease in the coefficient measuring the effect of the vote in the previous election, which falls from .82 to .37 over the postwar period (equation not shown).

I argued in Chapters 2 and 3 that, while competition for seats held by incumbents has, by some measures, declined, competition for open seats has increased. Incumbents may have tightened control of their seats; their parties have not—rather the contrary. If open seats have become more competitive, then we should expect an increase in the quality of candidates in these races—and vice versa. With improved chances of victory, the out-party ought to field more high-quality challengers; with opportunities to take seats held by incumbents declining, we would expect an increasing concentration of high-quality candidates in the contests for open seats. This is precisely what has occurred. Figure 4.8 displays the increase in the percentage of experienced open-seat candidates representing both the party currently holding the seat and the out-party. Although the pattern is, as usual, noisy, a significant increase is evident in both cases (see equations 1 and 4 in Table 4.9). The increase in high-quality candidates fielded by the out-party has been steeper, more than doubling (from about 22% to about 47%) over the postwar period.

Recall from the regression equations in Table 4.8 that the quality of the out-party's candidate has a greater impact on the vote and on who wins or loses. This implies that the trends displayed in Figure 4.8 should, other things equal, have made open seats more competitive, which is just what we observed. We cannot from these data untangle cause and effect. A more competitive environment should attract stronger candidates to open-seat contests; stronger candidates should make these contests more competitive. What we observe is the consequence of a mutually reinforcing set of processes: more competition in contests for open seats.

There are notable partisan differences in the incidence of high-quality candidates in contests for open House seats. An increased concentration of experienced candidates in open seats is characteristic of both parties, regardless of which party currently holds the seat. The difference is that Republicans are more likely than Democrats to field experienced candidates when they already hold the seat, while Democrats are more likely than Republicans to field experienced candidates when the other party currently holds the seat. The percentage of experienced Democrats has also grown faster than the percentage of experienced Republicans in such contests. The regression slopes on time from the equations in Table 4.9 indicate that the expected percentage of experienced out-party Democrats increased from 28.5% to 59.4% over the period, while the same figure for out-party Republicans grew from 17.8% to 36.3%. The increase in the quality of in-party candidates was nearly identical for both parties, rising from 58.4% to 77.5% for Republicans and from 52.0% to 70.7% for Democrats.

The comparatively low quality of Republican candidates for open seats that the Democrats currently hold probably contributes to the Republicans' inability to take more open seats from Democrats (see Chapter 3), because the effects of quality on election results are identical for the two parties (the coefficients on quality in the models estimated in Table 4.8 are not distinguishable by party). Clearly, Democrats have done the better job of fielding experienced candidates able to exploit the changes that have given parties greater access to each other's open seats.

THE CONCENTRATION OF COMPETITION

Several strands of evidence point to the conclusion that competition for House seats has become ever more concentrated in a smaller number of more intensely contested districts over the past two decades. High-

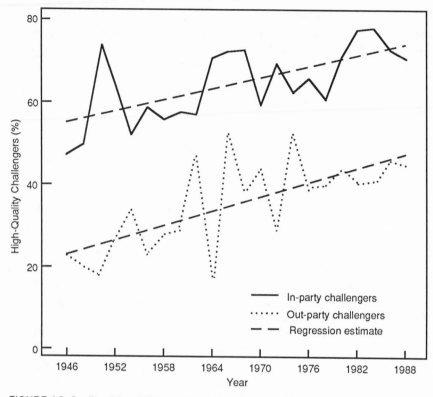

FIGURE 4.8 Quality of Candidates for Open House Seats, 1946–1988

TABLE 4.9
Increase in Quality of Candidates for Open House Seats, 1946–1988

Variables	In-Party Candidates			Out-Party Candidates		
	All (1)	Democrats (2)	Republicans (3)	All (4)	Democrats (5)	Republicans (6)
Intercept	53.56***	51.13***	57.45***	21.48***	27.13***	16.89***
	(3.11)	(5.36)	(4.74)	(3.57)	(5.56)	(4.38)
Election year	.92***	.89*	.91*	1.17***	1.46**	.88**
	(.24)	(.40)	(.36)	(.27)	(.42)	(.33)
Adjusted R^2	.40	.15	.20	.46	.34	.22
Durbin-Watson	1.64	1.83	1.97	3.07	2.43	2.66
Number of cases	22	22	22	22	22	22

*$p < .05$, one-tailed test.
**$p < .01$, one-tailed test.
***$p < .001$, one-tailed test.

Note: The dependent variable is the percentage of candidates for open seats in each category who have held elective office; the value of "election year" is 1946 = 1, 1948 = 2, . . . 1988 = 22; standard errors are in parentheses.

quality candidates are increasingly clustered in contests for open seats. Campaign money, too, is increasingly concentrated in open seats; recall from Figure 4.7 that spending by candidates for open seats has grown steeply since 1972, while spending by challengers has, in real terms, scarcely grown at all. Another perspective on this trend is presented in Figures 4.9 and 4.10, which trace changes in the distribution of campaign money available to nonincumbent House candidates. Figure 4.9 shows that the share of total spending accounted for by the top one-tenth of spenders rose steadily, from less than 30% to nearly 50%, between 1972 and 1988. In the meantime, the share spent by the lowest-spending six-tenths fell from 30% to less than 10%. Figure 4.10, which includes only challengers to incumbents, shows a similar pattern of change.

Why have campaign resources become so much more concentrated? A reflexive reference to the incumbency advantage will not suffice. The trend occurred after the mid-1960s, when the value of incumbency, in votes, had already had its sharpest increase; it continued regardless of whether the election year was particularly bad for one party's incumbents. Indeed, causation probably runs more strongly in the opposite direction: Concentration of resources raises the average incumbent's vote.

Although my view is admittedly speculative, I think the principal reasons for the growing concentration of campaign resources are better intelligence and higher campaign costs. Technology has reduced the cost of polling, and more money is available to pay for polls. The national party campaign committees have been particularly aggressive in exploring the prospects for taking particular seats from the opposition (Herrnson 1988). District electorates are subject to much more research than before, both prior to and during election campaigns. Thus strategic politicians and their potential supporters and contributors are better informed about the prospects for success than ever before. With a more refined idea of the possibilities, fewer resources are wasted on hopeless causes, and more are channeled into the tightest races.

The high price of competitive campaigns also leads to a bifurcation of effort. The costs in money, time, energy, privacy, and family life of a serious challenge are formidable and growing; the level of commitment necessary to take on an incumbent has grown with the length and cost of campaigns. Unless a potential candidate can convince him- or herself—and others—that he or she has a fighting chance and so can raise the very large sums needed to *have* a fighting chance, there is little point in making the other sacrifices a candidacy entails.

It is easy to understand how greater concentration of campaign resources would increase the incumbency advantage as it is customarily measured. A large majority of incumbents, appearing very safe indeed, face increasingly feeble opposition—or no major-party opposition at

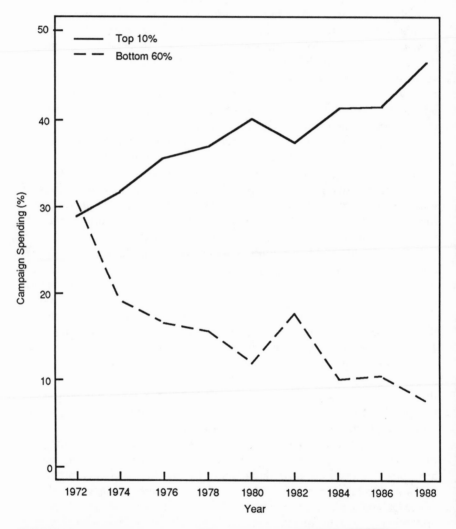

FIGURE 4.9 Growing Concentration of Campaign Money Spent by Nonincumbent House Candidates, 1972–1988

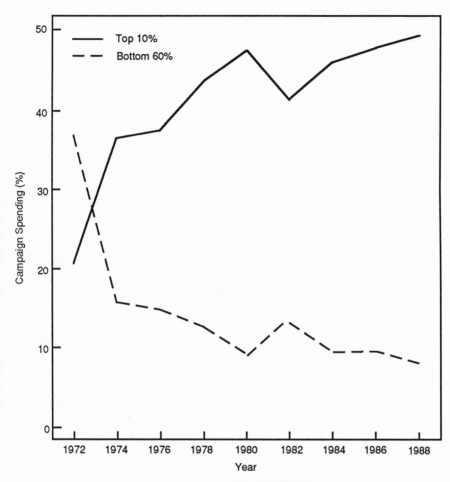

FIGURE 4.10 Growing Concentration of Campaign Money Spent by House Challengers, 1972–1988

all—and so win by even larger margins than before. Those who show signs of weakness continue to face full-scale challenges resulting in hard-fought, close races, some of which they lose. The average vote for incumbents grows, but this does not represent an increase in the value of incumbency *to those incumbents who are seriously challenged.* Concentration of resources makes incumbents who convince the opposition that they are unbeatable even safer (by the criterion of vote margin), but it also makes life more difficult for incumbents who appear sufficiently vulnerable to invite an all-out challenge.

The concentration of resources may, however, diminish competition and protect incumbents by prematurely closing off the possibility of a competitive challenge. Election forecasts made months in advance of election day are subject to considerable error; bleak prospects can suddenly brighten if national or local events break for the challenger. Voters do change their minds during the course of campaigns (Jacobson 1990b). More challenges may appear hopeless than turns out to be the case; too much information, too early, may discourage the kind of risk taking that is occasionally rewarded with unanticipated success.

CONCLUSION

As the electoral importance of incumbency grew over the postwar period, so did the electoral importance of the opposing campaign, and for the very same reasons. With a growing fraction of the electorate choosing between candidates rather than parties, the individual characteristics of candidates and their campaigns became more salient. Just as what incumbents did in office could have an increasing impact on their support in the district, so could the persona and message of the challenger.

The quality of challengers and vigor of their campaigns are more variable than partisan habits, and so their increasing impact also helps to explain why interelection vote swings have become more variable and election results less stable over the period (see Chapter 2). It also points to a major reason Republicans have not done better in the most recent House elections: They have fielded comparatively inexperienced, underfinanced, nonincumbent candidates.

NOTES

1. To be sure, primary elections and independent candidacies may offer some choice, but their contribution to electoral competition in postwar House elections has been limited; incumbents are four times more likely to be defeated in general than in primary elections.

2. The South is defined as the eleven states of the Confederacy: Alabama, Arkansas, Florida, Georgia, Louisiana, Mississippi, North Carolina, South Carolina, Tennessee, Texas, and Virginia.

3. In addition to local newspapers (the Library of Congress has on microfilm at least two newspapers from each state) and all of the *Congressional Quarterly Weekly Report's* reviews of individual House races since Congressional Quarterly, Inc., began publishing them, background information on candidates comes from *Election Index* (1966, 1968, 1970, 1972, 1974, 1976, 1978, 1980, 1982), *Biographical Directory of the American Congress* (1971), various regional and occupational editions of *Who's Who*, the *New York Times* (using the obituary index as well as

the regular index), various state election pamphlets, and numerous other mis-cellaneous sources. I also checked state yearbooks to determine whether any of the candidates about whom I could find no information had held any state office; for some states, lists of local elected officials were also available for examination. About 5% of the cases remain uncertain from lack of information (some highly partisan newspapers did not even deign to mention the names of losing candidates representing the unworthy party). I have assumed that these candidates had not held elective public office. Given their obscurity and that only about one-quarter of the known challengers have held elective office, the number of errors produced by this assumption should be quite small; overall accuracy probably exceeds 99%. In any case, all of the substantive results are replicated if the definition of high-quality candidates is narrowed to include only candidates who have held seats in state legislatures or, formerly, the U.S. Congress; for this classification, information is virtually complete and errors minimal.

4. See also Bianco (1984); Bond, Covington, and Fleisher (1985); Canon (1985); and Krasno and Green (1988).

5. All candidates are assumed to have spent a minimum of $5,000. I make this assumption for two reasons. One is that expenditures totalling less than this sum need not be reported to the Federal Election Commission. The second is that the assumption produces results that closely approximate those attained when the Box-Cox procedure is used to find the appropriate functional form for modeling the diminishing returns on campaign spending; see Jacobson (1990b) for the details. The spending data are from Common Cause (1974, 1976); the Federal Election Commission (1979, 1982, 1983, 1985); and Barone and Ujifusa (1987, 1989).

6. The positive sign on the election year variable indicates that, while the impact of the prior vote has diminished, the challenger's share of the vote independent of the prior vote has actually increased. The net effect of these two trends puts challengers in a worse position, however, unless the prior vote is less than 16%.

7. The data to compute quarter-to-quarter changes in real income per capita through 1976 are from *The National Income and Product Accounts of the United States, 1929–76, Statistical Tables* (U.S. Department of Commerce, 1981). Data for later years are taken from various issues of *The Survey of Current Business* (U.S. Department of Commerce). Year-to-year changes are computed from data in *The Economic Report of the President, 1989*. Quarterly data are not available for 1945–1946, so the yearly figure is substituted for that observation for analyses reported in Tables 4.5 and 4.6.

8. Presidential approval data are from King and Ragsdale (1988).

9. Of course, decisions to run for Congress are sometimes taken months or even years earlier (Maisel 1982; Born 1986)—though most nonincumbent House candidates do not register with the Federal Election Commission until March of the election year or later (Wilcox 1987; Wilcox and Biersack 1990). The choice of a time frame over which to measure for real income change makes little difference, however; all of the plausible alternatives are so highly correlated that it is impossible to distinguish alternative models statistically (Erikson 1990a).

10. I set the minimum value of this variable at 0, which is the natural logarithm of 1, because the log of 0 (the actual ratio for Republicans in some Southern states prior to the 1960s) is undefined.

11. Regional differences in the quality of Democratic challengers have disappeared. In the 1950s and 1960s, experienced Democratic challengers were somewhat more common in the South—not surprising at a time when local offices were monopolized by Democrats, and Republican incumbents seemed aberrant and therefore relatively easy targets. Since the 1960s, the proportion of experienced Democratic challengers has not differed by region.

5

Democratic Hegemony in the House: Structural Explanations

During the spring of 1989, critics of the "ossified" Congress took delight in pointing out that a far larger proportion of incumbents were defeated in the Soviet Union's first free elections to the Congress of Peoples' Deputies than in the 1988 U.S. House elections. Former president Ronald Reagan complained that there was "less turnover in Congress than in the Supreme Soviet" (*Washington Post*, May 24, 1989, B3:4). The rhetorical point was that House incumbents have become so entrenched, competition for House seats so one-sided, that the makeup of Congress is less responsive to public preferences than the makeup of the Soviet legislature. David Mayhew's concern that the "vanishing marginals" signalled the "blunting of a blunt instrument" (1974b:314), with congressional elections losing their capacity to enforce collective responsibility, seemed prescient. Republicans, out to change the rules, agreed: Structural barriers prevented them from winning a share of House seats fairly reflecting their support in the electorate.

In this chapter, I examine the evidence for these views. I first consider whether House election results have, in fact, become less responsive to national political events and conditions and so, by implication, to changes in voters' preferences. I then consider whether Republican candidates in particular have suffered from structural changes in the electoral process. I conclude that none of the common structural explanations for continued Democratic hegemony in the House—including a declining swing-ratio, gerrymandering, and campaign finance regulation—withstands serious analysis. The sources of Republican failures and thus of divided control must lie elsewhere.

NATIONAL TIDES IN HOUSE ELECTIONS

The peculiar structure of the American political system has never made it easy for voters to hold elected leaders collectively responsible for the government's performance. Where votes are cast to choose a governing party, and only incidentally particular legislators, as in most parliamentary systems, enforcement of collective responsibility is relatively uncomplicated, and so incentives for members of governing parties to pursue successful national policies are unambiguous. Where executives and legislatures are elected separately, however, legislators can contemplate independent electoral careers. Insofar as personal ties to constituents protect them from punishment by association for bad times or failed programs, incentives for producing collectively beneficial policies are weakened. Elections that revolve around local candidates and issues, slighting national parties and leaders, reward individual responsiveness at the expense of collective responsibility (Fiorina 1980; Jacobson 1987b).

Despite the formal separation of congressional from presidential elections, the historic pattern of House seat swings suggests that, by using party labels to assign credit or blame for national conditions, voters have been able to enforce a considerable degree of collective responsibility. Historically, unpopular presidents or presidential candidates, unpopular or failed national policies, and poor economic performance have all cost the administration's party seats in Congress. Successful presidents and policies have, in the short term as well as in the long run, added to the party's congressional strength.

Whether this is still true is a valid question. Have electoral results become less responsive to national conditions over the postwar period? Some of the evidence discussed in previous chapters would lead us to believe that responsiveness has diminished. Electoral disaggregation, especially the increasing dissociation of presidential from other election results, implies a diminished electoral role for national forces. But it is important to avoid confusing electoral articulation at the district level with electoral articulation at higher levels of aggregation. The relationship between U.S. House elections and state legislative elections provides a good illustration of this point. Recall from Table 2.2 in Chapter 2 that the impact of the partisan distribution of state legislative seats on the probability of a party's winning a given House seat in the state has fallen sharply over the postwar period. The connection has diminished to the point where the distribution of state legislative seats in the average House Democrat's state is only slightly more Democratic than the distribution of state legislative seats in the average House Republican's state.[1]

On a district-by-district, state-by-state basis, the link between the outcomes of state legislative and House elections has become remarkably weak. In aggregate, however, these sets of elections continue to move together with considerable precision, as Figure 5.1 demonstrates. The entries are the percentage of House seats won by Democrats and the mean percentage of Democrats elected to the lower house of the state legislature. At the highest level of aggregation, House and state legislative elections continue to track one another quite closely. And they have done so just as closely in the second half of this period as they did in the first, as the regression equations in Table 5.1 indicate. The only notable difference between the equations for the two periods is the intercept, which tells us that, controlling for the aggregate House results, aggregate state legislative results have been *more* favorable to Democrats during the period of Republican presidential hegemony. Dissociation between individual elections does not, then, necessarily mean a decoupling of aggregate electoral results across offices; it does not preclude strong and consistent national electoral change across a range of offices in response to national conditions.

The search for systematic evidence that national conditions shape aggregate election results has produced a literature far too large to review comprehensively here. It contains numerous points of disagreement fueled by differences in models, analytic methods, and time periods, but until recently the findings have generally supported the conventional wisdom: The public's view of presidents and presidential candidates and the performance of the national economy have an important influence on congressional election results (Kramer 1971; Arcelus and Meltzer 1975; Bloom and Price 1975; and Tufte 1975, 1978). Some scholars have recently claimed that economic conditions have not affected postwar House elections (Alesina and Rosenthal 1989), at least not at the midterm (Erikson 1990a), but small and reasonable re-specifications of their models produce results consistent with the notion that the economy does indeed matter.[2] The question remains, however, as to whether the effects of national conditions as measured by these models have declined over the postwar period.

The regression equations reported in Table 5.2 present part of the answer. The model I estimate is typical of the genre (Tufte 1975). The dependent variable is the change in the percentage of seats held by the administration's party before and after the election. I control for the party's "exposure"—the percentage of seats it holds above or below its moving average over the eight previous elections (Oppenheimer, Stimson, and Waterman 1986). The variables measuring national conditions are the change in real per capita income in the year preceding the election and the president's level of popular approval in the last Gallup Poll taken prior to the election.[3]

The first equation in Table 5.2 covers the entire postwar period. All of the variables work as expected, and their coefficients are significant at p < .01 or better.[4] According to these coefficients, the difference between the lowest and highest values of presidential approval translates

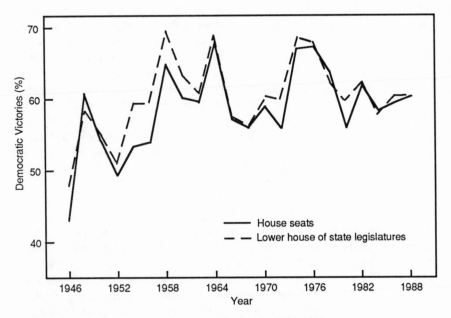

FIGURE 5.1 House Seats and State Legislative Seats, 1946–1988

TABLE 5.1
Aggregate State Legislative Results and Aggregate House Election Results, 1946–1988

Variable	1946–1966 (1)	1968–1988 (2)
Intercept	10.78*	13.38*
	(5.11)	(6.81)
House seats won by Democrats (%)	.81***	.80***
	(.09)	(.11)
Adjusted R^2	.89	.83
Durbin-Watson	1.60	2.11
Number of cases	11	11

*p < .05, one-tailed test.
***p < .001, one-tailed test.

Note: The dependent variable is the percentage of seats won by Democrats in all lower-house state legislative elections nationally; standard errors are in parentheses.

TABLE 5.2
Effects of National Conditions on House Elections, 1946–1988

Variable	1946–1988 (1)	1946–1966 (2)	1968–1988 (3)
Intercept	−19.54***	−27.64**	−6.55
	(4.50)	(7.19)	(4.08)
Exposure	−.62***	−.80***	−.31
	(.13)	(.19)	(.18)
Change in real income per capita (%)	1.31**	1.55*	1.53***
	(.39)	(.62)	(.35)
Presidential approval (%)	.28**	.41**	.02
	(.09)	(.13)	(.09)
Adjusted R^2	.64	.67	.79
Durbin-Watson	2.49	2.44	2.67
Number of cases	22	11	11

*p < .05, one-tailed test.
**p < .01, one-tailed test.
***p < .001, one-tailed test.

Note: See the text for a description of the variables; standard errors are in parentheses.

into a difference of 52 seats, and the difference between the lowest and highest values of real per capita income change translates into a difference of 49 seats. The remaining two equations cover 1946–1966 and 1968–1988, respectively. Real income change has the same effect in both periods, but the coefficient on presidential approval drops from .41 to .02, and the difference between the two is significant (p < .05, according to the interaction term; the difference in the exposure parameter is not significant by this standard).

The change is not so large, and the difference is not statistically significant, if we assume that, in 1974, voters were responding more to Richard Nixon's presidency than to Gerald Ford's and replace Ford's approval rating with Nixon's much lower final rating. The coefficient on presidential approval for the 1968–1988 period becomes .24 with a standard error of .08. Still, it appears that presidential approval, though not the economy, has had a smaller impact on aggregate House election results in recent elections.

Superficially, Democrats appear to have benefitted from a decline in the impact of presidential approval on aggregate House election results. The average final approval rating of the Democratic presidents in office during the 1968–1988 period was 42%, that of Republican presidents, 54%. To be sure, Republicans were protected in 1982, when Ronald Reagan's approval hit its all-time low of 42% just before the election, but they could not benefit from a relatively high level of presidential approval in the 1984, 1986, and 1988 elections (58%, 63%, and 54%, respectively).

In a more basic sense, however, these findings simply underline the disjunction that is a major focus of this book: Successful Republican presidencies have not added much to the party's strength in Congress. This result thus begs the question rather than answering it. The economy's influence remains as strong as before, indicating that national conditions continue to shape aggregate House results. Notice also that more of the variance in aggregate seat swings is explained by national conditions in the later than in the earlier period (adjusted R^2's of .79 and .67, respectively).

PRESIDENTIAL COATTAILS REVISITED

The presidential contest is the other well-studied national source of influence on aggregate congressional election outcomes. The growing separation of presidential and House election outcomes at the district level was documented in Chapter 2. As we noted, this change does not preclude a continuing connection between individual voters' presidential and congressional vote decisions. It also does not preclude coattail effects in the aggregate (recall Figure 5.1). It is possible for aggregate congressional results to track national presidential results even though the presidential winner is a poor predictor of the House winner in any particular district.

The literature offers conflicting findings on whether aggregate coattail effects have in fact declined over the postwar period. John Ferejohn and Randall Calvert (1984) present evidence that coattails have indeed atrophied, with the presidential vote having a smaller effect on aggregate House results in the postwar period than in earlier eras, and a smaller effect in the period 1968–1980 than 1952–1964. They perform no tests of significance, however, and their results depend on regression equations with as few as four observations, so their findings are scarcely definitive. James E. Campbell's (1986) model suggests that the impact of the presidential vote on House seat swings was higher from 1900 to 1940 (1% of the presidential vote was worth 4.25 seats) than from 1944 through 1980 (1% of the presidential vote translating into 3.22 seats), but he does not test for a change in this parameter over the postwar period.

Campbell's model regresses the change in the number of seats won by Democrats in the House on the average number of seats they won in the previous two elections (which Campbell calls the "base"), the Democratic presidential candidate's share of the two-party vote, and an interaction term registering a change in the effect of the base after 1964.

TABLE 5.3
Decline of Presidential Coattails, 1948–1988

Variable	(1)
Intercept	160.03***
	(37.62)
Base	−1.64***
	(.16)
Post-1964	106.00*
	(37.58)
Democratic presidential vote (%)	5.04***
	(.52)
Democratic presidential vote (%) × post-1964	−1.53*
	(.79)
Adjusted R²	.95
Durbin-Watson	1.88
Number of cases	11

*p < .05, one-tailed test.
***p < .001, one-tailed test.

Note: See the text for a description of the variables; standard errors are in parentheses.

This interaction may pick up some of the decline in coattail effects, so I replace it with an interaction term registering a change in the effect of the presidential vote after 1964. Estimates of this model for postwar elections are listed in Table 5.3. The coefficients show a statistically significant decline of about 30% in the effect of the presidential vote; 1% of the two-party presidential vote was "worth" 5.04 House seats in the 1948–1964 period, 3.51 seats thereafter. This finding must be taken with more than a few grains of salt, however, because it rests on so few observations (eleven), and the degrees of freedom are perilously low. Still, it is consistent with the view that during the period of Republican presidential hegemony, presidential coattails have not proven as productive of House seats as they were prior to 1968. Again, however, this is precisely the kind of change we would expect to underlie an era of divided government. It describes but does not explain what has happened.

Whether or not the impact of national forces on aggregate House election results has diminished, it has become more contingent, depending to a greater degree on the strategic decisions of potential candidates and contributors (Jacobson and Kernell 1983; Jacobson 1989). National conditions continue to create problems or opportunities for congressional candidates (Jacobson and Kernell 1990), but how these problems are handled or exploited makes more difference now than in the past (see

Chapter 4). When a party does not field enough challengers with the resources and skills to take full advantage of the opportunities created by national conditions, partisan swings may indeed be dampened (Jacobson 1985a, 1989). But this does not mean that aggregate election results have lost the potential to respond to national conditions as strongly as they did forty years ago. I will have more to say about this in the next chapter.

TRANSLATING VOTES INTO SEATS

A common explanation for the declining influence of presidential politics on aggregate House election results, to the specific detriment of the Republican party, is that the enlarged incumbency advantage has dampened the translation of changes in voters' preferences into changes in party control of House seats (Born 1984). As I argued in Chapter 3, this change could scarcely be the full explanation for the Republicans' failure to win more House seats, because 90% of House seats have been open at one time or another since 1968. Still, it is possible that an enlarged incumbency advantage has made it more difficult for Republicans—or Democrats, for that matter—to take as much advantage of strong short-term forces favoring their party's candidates. And if incumbency protects House members from the consequences of strong national swings against their party, the distribution of House seats can no longer accurately reflect changes in voter sentiment.

The translation of votes into seats is commonly measured by the "swing ratio"—the share of seats a party adds for a unit increase in its share of votes. Mayhew (1974b) expected the "vanishing marginals" to reduce the responsiveness of seat swings to vote swings, and some scholars (Ansolabehere, Brady, and Fiorina 1989; Fiorina 1989) have subsequently reported dramatic drops in the swing ratio, though others (Ferejohn and Calvert 1984; Jacobson 1987a) have demurred. In this section I argue that the swing ratio has declined, at most, only modestly and that the difference this has made in the distribution of House seats is probably quite small. In particular, I show that the sensitivity of seat shifts to vote shifts in districts contested by *challengers* favored by national tides has diminished very little. The problem is, rather, that *vote* swings in these districts have diminished. The growing difference between the magnitudes of vote swings to incumbents and challengers of the favored party suggests that the very concept of a "national tide" in House elections has become problematic, robbing the swing ratio, as it is customarily conceived, of meaning. The undoubted decline in turnover of House seats in recent elections does not, then, stand as evidence that the electorate's will has been thwarted by the electoral process or that the House is immune to changes in public sentiments.

ESTIMATING THE SWING RATIO

The swing ratio measures the translation of votes into seats in legislative elections. For postwar House elections, the dependent variable is unproblematic: 435 seats were at stake in every election save 1958 (436) and 1960 (437), and virtually every winner was either a Republican or a Democrat. The proportion of seats won or gained by a party is thus the obvious choice.

The measure of votes, in contrast, remains unsettled, and substantive results vary according to the alternative chosen. Most studies have measured a party's vote as its percentage share of the total votes cast nationwide for major-party candidates (Tufte 1973; Ferejohn and Calvert 1984; Jacobson 1987a). Stephen Ansolabehere, David W. Brady, and Morris P. Fiorina, drawing on the analysis of Graham Gudgin and Peter Taylor (1979), argue that the party's mean district vote is a superior measure on the ground that it is the "relevant determinant of the probability that a seat switches party control" (1988:12) and that it is a superior estimator of the underlying distribution of partisan preferences. Even conceding their point, Gudgin and Taylor's observation that "if the national strength of a party is of interest, then the figure to use is the overall proportion of the vote" (quoted in Ansolabehere, Brady, and Fiorina 1988:11) remains valid. It makes perfect sense to use the national vote to measure partisan preferences if the point is to discover the relationship between the support a party enjoys nationally and its share of House seats, a relationship of obvious relevance to arguments about the democratic responsiveness of the electoral system.

The difference between these two measures would be of little substantive importance were it not for another problem: variation in the number of uncontested seats. When seats are uncontested, the (potential) votes for at least one party are left out of national totals; occasionally the winner's votes are not recorded, and even when they are, the total may be considerably less than it would have been had the outcome not already been determined. Uncontested seats therefore contribute imprecision to the national vote as a measure of national partisan preferences. They also distort the underlying distribution that the mean district vote is supposed to estimate. If one party holds more uncontested seats than the other, omitting them from calculations underestimates its strength, while including them valued at 100% overestimates its strength. This would not be so important if the relative number of uncontested seats

TABLE 5.4
Models of Swing Ratio in House Elections, 1946–1988

| | Vote Measure | | | |
| | National Vote Division | Mean District Vote (contested seats only) | Mean District Vote (all seats) | |
Variable	(1)	(2)	(3)	(4)
Intercept	−38.76***	−48.30***	−16.83	−71.16***
	(7.98)	(7.58)	(22.13)	(12.25)
Democrats' vote share (%)	1.83***	2.03***	1.29**	2.47***
	(.15)	(.14)	(.38)	(.23)
Party difference in unopposed seats				−.29***
				(.03)
Adjusted R^2	.88	.90	.34	.85
Durbin-Watson	1.51	1.86	.62	1.65
Mean residual in seats:				
1946–1964	−.33	−1.78	−14.60	−2.64
1966–1988	.27	1.48	12.17	2.21
Number of cases	22	22	22	22

**p < .01, one-tailed test.
***p < .001, one-tailed test.

Note: The dependent variable is the Democrats' percentage of House seats; the independent variables are various measures of the percentage share of the two-party vote for Democrats (see the text); "party difference in unopposed seats" is the number of unopposed Democrats minus the number of unopposed Republicans, unopposed defined as having no major-party opponent in the general election; standard errors are in parentheses.

were stable or varied randomly over time; but, as we saw in Figure 4.1, it does not.

The usual way to estimate the swing ratio is to regress seat shares on vote shares over a series of elections; the regression coefficient estimates the swing ratio.[5] Because none of the vote measures is without flaws or obviously superior to the rest, the prudent strategy is to compare results from several of the leading candidates. Insofar as the findings are consistent despite differences in how the vote is measured, the problem, for practical purposes, is solved.

Table 5.4 reports the results using three alternative measures of the vote. The first equation uses the national vote; the second, the mean two-party vote in districts with major party competition; and the remaining two, the mean two-party vote across all districts (with unopposed winners assigned 100%).

The results from the first two equations in Table 5.4 are quite similar; the mean absolute difference in Democratic seat shares predicted by the two is 1.4 percentage points. Examination of the residuals (translated into numbers of seats) from both equations indicates that they tend to underestimate the effects of a unit vote shift during the first part of the postwar period (1946–1964) and overestimate its effects in the second part (1966–1988), lending credence to the idea that the Democrats benefitted when incumbents' electoral margins rose. But note that the differences are exceedingly small, amounting to at most a couple of seats.

This is not at all true of the third equation, which replicates Ansolabehere, Brady, and Fiorina's analysis (with 1988 added). Its residuals suggest that dramatic changes have taken place, with the equation underestimating the Democrats' share by an average of 15 seats over the first period and overestimating it by an average of 12 seats during the more recent period. But these results are severely contaminated by the secular change in the relative number of uncontested Democratic and Republican seats. The Democrats' advantage in uncontested seats has declined over time, reducing their mean district vote (when unopposed victors are assigned 100%) quite independently of any other change. Recall from Chapter 4 that the biggest change came in the early 1960s, with the surge of Republican activity in the South. Prior to 1966, Democrats had an average of 67 more uncontested victories than did Republicans; since 1966, their advantage has dropped to an average of 40.

The kind of distortion this change can produce is evident when we compare Ansolabehere, Brady, and Fiorina's measure with the other measures—and our intuitions—in particular years. According to their measure, House Democrats won more support in 1960 (a mean district vote of 61.5%), when their representation fell 21 seats to 262, than they did in 1964 (61.2%), when they added 37 seats to reach their postwar high of 295. But this circumstance is strictly an artifact of changes in the number of uncontested seats: Democrats won 72 more uncontested seats than did Republicans in 1960; in 1964, the difference was reduced to 40. The national two-party vote rose from 54.8% to 57.3% between the two elections; the mean Democratic vote in contested districts increased from 53.5% to 57.1%. Clearly, the latter two measures give a much more accurate picture of changes in the electorate's preferences between the two elections.

The decline in the Democrats' lead in uncontested seats over time explains why the fit of equation 3 is so poor, relative to the others (adjusted $R^2 = .34$, compared to .88 and .90, respectively, for the first two equations), and why it suffers from serially correlated errors (Durbin-Watson $= .62$). When the party difference in uncontested seats is taken into account, as in equation 4, the fit is improved dramatically, errors cease to be correlated, and the equation produces results much closer to those in equations 1 and 2. Again, comparison of the residuals for

TABLE 5.5
Change in Swing Ratio for House Elections, 1946–1988

Variable	National Vote Division (1)	Mean District Vote (contested seats only) (2)	Mean District Vote (all seats) (3)	(4)
Intercept	−48.53*** (10.25)	−57.22*** (9.16)	−74.55** (23.57)	−92.97*** (14.39)
Democrats' vote share (%)	2.01*** (.20)	2.19*** (.18)	2.20*** (.40)	2.77*** (.26)
Post-1964	27.54 (17.05)	29.34* (15.31)	53.57 (33.09)	43.73* (19.79)
Post-1964 × Democrats' vote share (%)	−.51 (.32)	−.54* (.29)	−.79 (.57)	−.70* (.34)
Party difference in unopposed seats				−.24*** (.04)
Adjusted R^2	.88	.91	.69	.89
Durbin-Watson	1.42	2.05	1.82	2.08
Number of cases	22	22	22	22

*p < .05, one-tailed test.
**p < .01, one-tailed test.
***p < .001, one-tailed test.

Note: The dependent variable is the Democrats' percentage of House seats; the independent variables are various measures of the percentage share of the two-party vote for Democrats (see the text); "post-1964" takes the value of 1 if the election year is 1966 or later, 0 otherwise; standard errors are in parentheses.

the two time periods indicates a quite modest change in the expected share of seats Democrats win with a given share of the vote.

CHANGES IN THE SWING RATIO

A more precise view of how the swing ratio has changed, and what difference this may have made for congressional representation, is provided by equations that measure change explicitly. The equations in Table 5.5 estimate the change in the swing ratio between the two periods by including a dummy variable to distinguish the periods and allowing it to interact with the vote measure.[6] This is, of course, equivalent to estimating separate equations for each time period. The first two equations reveal a statistically significant (p < .05, one-tailed) decrease of about 25% in the swing coefficient between the two periods. But notice that the constant term increases sharply as well; this has the effect of reducing the impact of the parameter shift on the actual distribution of seats.

The third equation replicates (with the addition of 1988) Ansolabehere, Brady, and Fiorina's analysis of the parameter shift. Their model shows a larger (36%) though more imprecisely measured decline in the swing ratio. On the basis of this parameter shift, Fiorina argues that "If the marginals had not declined in number and congressional elections had remained as susceptible to national tides as they were a generation ago, then, all other things equal, the Republicans would have taken majorities of House seats five times since the mid-1960s" (1989:136). These are startling results and, if accepted, certainly justify the Republicans' sense of having been unfairly denied a share of House seats commensurate with their growing strength in the electorate. But the estimates are, once again, distorted by changes in the distribution of uncontested seats. When this variable is taken into account (equation 4), the Republican majorities disappear; the fit also improves markedly and again the equation suggests a more modest 25% decline in the swing ratio.

The projected effects of changes in the swing regimes on the number of House seats Democrats have won since 1966 are displayed in Table 5.6. The table lists the actual number of seats won by Democrats in elections since 1966 and the numbers predicted by the equation for the entire postwar period (from Table 5.4) and the parameters estimated for the 1946–1964 period (from Table 5.5) applied to the 1966–1988 period, for each measure of the Democrats' vote.

Only Ansolabehere, Brady, and Fiorina's original model projects dramatic differences, with Republican majorities in 1966, 1968, 1972, 1980, and 1984. With few exceptions, the results from the other models indicate that the distribution of House seats since 1966 would have been little different under the old swing regime. Democratic dominance would have continued. In no election would the Republicans have been predicted to win a majority, though they would have come considerably closer in 1966, 1968, and 1984, especially if we believe the parameters from equation 4 in Table 5.4. In general, however, predicted seat divisions are not much different when parameters are allowed to change. The average number of net seats changing hands would have been somewhat greater, but with the big differences concentrated in a few elections, notably 1970, 1984, and 1986. This is not accidental, as we shall see.

From this perspective, the enhanced incumbency advantage in House elections has had an observable but surprisingly modest effect on congressional representation. Certainly Republicans cannot blame the "vanishing marginals" for denying them the just fruits of changes in the preferences expressed by House voters. But this is not the only valid perspective. Ansolabehere, Brady, and Fiorina note that "the vanishing marginals literature is primarily about incumbents and the changes taking place in incumbent contested elections" (1988:14) and proceed to estimate

TABLE 5.6
Democratic House Seats Predicted by Models of Swing Ratio, 1966–1988

| | | National Vote Division | | Mean District Vote (contested only) | | | Mean District Vote (including uncontested) | | |
Year	Actual Seats	(1a)	(1b)	(2a)	(2b)	(3a)	(3b)	(4a)	(4b)
						Seats Predicted by:			
1966	248	239	238	234	231	242	212*	234	223
1968	243	236	234	239	236	233	198*	237	221
1970	255	263	264	260	260	258	241	260	254
1972	243	250	250	248	246	241	211*	248	233
1974	291	296	301	296	298	280	277	293	293
1976	292	286	289	287	288	264	251	287	279
1978	277	264	265	272	272	249	226	276	262
1980	243	238	237	247	245	233	197*	249	230
1982	268	274	282	273	273	254	233	273	262
1984	253	249	249	237	234	236	203*	235	219
1986	258	268	270	265	265	250	227	265	252
1988	260	260	261	256	257	246	220	251	239
Mean	261	260	261	259	259	248	225	259	247

| | | National Vote Division | | Mean District Vote (contested only) | | | Mean District Vote (including uncontested) | | |
Year	Actual Change	(1a)	(1b)	(2a)	(2b)	(3a)	(3b)	(4a)	(4b)
						Net Seat Change Predicted by:			
1966	47	47	52	60	65	29	50	66	72
1968	5	3	4	5	5	8	14	3	2
1970	12	27	30	21	24	25	43	23	33
1972	12	13	14	12	14	18	30	12	21
1974	49	46	51	48	52	39	66	45	60
1976	1	10	12	9	10	16	27	6	14
1978	15	22	24	15	16	14	25	11	17
1980	34	26	28	25	27	17	29	27	32
1982	25	36	45	26	28	21	36	24	32
1984	14	25	33	36	39	18	31	38	43
1986	5	19	21	28	31	14	24	30	33
1988	2	8	11	9	8	4	7	14	13
Mean	18	24	27	25	27	19	32	25	31

*Republican majority.

Note: Column numbers refer to the equations in Tables 5.4 and 5.5 used to compute the estimates; estimates using the 1946–1964 parameters from the equations in Table 5.5 applied to the 1966–1988 elections are listed under the "b" columns.

TABLE 5.7
Vote Swing to Candidates of Party Gaining Votes, 1946–1988

Year	Party	National Swing	Mean District Swing	Mean Swing to: Incumbents	Challengers
1946	R	6.4	5.0	3.7	6.2
1948	D	8.0	7.4	6.7	7.8
1950	R	3.2	2.7	3.0	2.1
1952	R	0.1	2.5	2.1	2.7
1954	D	2.7	4.0	4.6	3.5
1956	R	1.6	2.1	1.9	2.6
1958	D	5.0	6.7	8.8	4.9
1960	R	1.2	2.9	2.5	3.4
1962	R	2.3	1.0	2.0	0.2
1964	D	4.8	5.0	5.0	5.0
1966	R	6.0	6.3	9.7	4.8
1968	R	0.4	0.2	1.8	−0.6
1970	D	3.4	3.4	5.5	1.8
1972	R	1.6	1.9	2.8	0.9
1974	D	5.8	6.7	6.5	7.2
1976	R	1.3	1.7	4.6	0.2
1978	R	2.8	1.9	4.5	1.2
1980	R	3.2	3.3	4.9	2.4
1982	D	5.2	3.2	3.3	3.5
1984	R	3.8	3.9	6.4	2.2
1986	D	2.4	3.3	5.7	0.9
1988	R	1.0	0.7	2.3	−0.2
Means:					
1946–1964		3.5	3.9	4.0	3.8
1966–1988		3.2	3.0	4.8	2.0

Note: Mean district swing and mean swings to incumbents and challengers of party gaining votes include only those contests with major party competition in the previous and current elections.

separate swing ratios for incumbent-held and open seats. They find that the swing ratio for incumbent-held seats was lower by more than 50% (.98 compared with 2.06) and that the ratio for open seats was more than twice as large (4.14 compared with 1.76), for 1966–1986 compared with 1946–1964.[7]

Ansolabehere, Brady, and Fiorina are right to direct our attention to contests involving incumbents, but they do not go far enough. For the focus should not be merely on seats held by incumbents, but on seats held by incumbents *of the party facing contrary national tides.* Swings of voter sentiment to a party's incumbents cannot give it additional seats; only swings to its challengers have this potential. With this in mind, observe the data in Table 5.7. The table lists the mean national swing, mean district swing, and mean swings to the incumbents and challengers of the party gaining votes in each election since 1946.

Table 5.7 reveals that, for the 1946–1964 period, average swings were balanced between incumbents and challengers. In five of the ten elections, the average challenger of the party gaining votes enjoyed a larger vote increase than did the party's average incumbent. Since 1964, however, incumbents have absorbed a greatly disproportionate share of the aggregate swing. In only two of the twelve elections has the swing to challengers been larger than the swing to incumbents (or the average swing across all contested districts), and these are, not coincidentally, years in which the winning party's seat gains tend to match predictions. In contrast, in those years for which the equations substantially overpredict the number of net seats that should switch party control—the aforementioned 1970, 1984, and 1986, for example—the swing to challengers is much less than the national swing, let alone the swing to incumbents of the favored party.

In light of these observations, the appropriate step is to estimate the swing ratio for those seats contested by challengers of the party favored by national trends. The results are in Table 5.8. The regression equations estimate the effects of mean district vote swings to challengers on two dependent variables: the percentage of total House seats gained by the party and the percentage of its challengers who defeated incumbents. Interaction terms measure changes in the swing ratios in the mid-1960s.

Although falling below conventional levels of statistical significance, the interaction coefficients again suggest that the swing ratio is about 25% lower for the more recent period; however, the upward shift in the intercept cancels whatever substantive impact this change may have had. Table 5.9 lists the actual and predicted net seat swings and incumbent defeats, with the parameters for the 1946–1964 period used to predict outcomes for 1966–1988 in the third and sixth columns. Whether the dependent variable is the overall seat swing or the percentage of incumbents defeated, there is no evidence that the swing regime in force in 1946–1964 would have increased turnover or expelled more incumbents. If anything, the parameters from the earlier period *underestimate* seat changes for the later period.

The point is clear: The responsiveness of seat swings to vote swings *to challengers* has changed little, if at all, with the vanishing of the marginals. As a group, incumbents are no more insulated from contrary shifts in district voter sentiment than they were prior to the mid-1960s. If House members are now harder to defeat, it is not because contrary vote swings have a diminished impact on seat swings, but rather because the contrary vote swings have themselves diminished. The very high rate of success enjoyed by incumbents in recent elections, particularly the last three, is anomalous only when viewed from the perspective of the national swings for all House candidates; it is not at all anomalous

TABLE 5.8
Swing Ratio for Challengers of Party Gaining Votes, 1946–1988

	Dependent Variable			
	Total Seats Added (%)		Incumbents Defeated (%)	
	(1)	(2)	(3)	(4)
Intercept	.09	−1.64	.91	−.60
	(.71)	(1.36)	(1.08)	(2.06)
Mean vote shift to challengers (%)	1.87***	2.25***	3.36***	3.85***
	(.19)	(.31)	(.29)	(.47)
Post-1964		2.39		2.23
		(1.59)		(2.40)
Post-1964 × mean vote shift to challengers (%)		−.59		−1.01
		(.42)		(.63)
Adjusted R²	.81	.82	.86	.87
Durbin-Watson	1.74	1.89	2.12	1.92
Number of cases	22	22	22	22

***p < .001, one-tailed test.

Note: The dependent variables are indicated by the column heads; the independent variables are the change in the mean percentage of the two-party vote won by challengers of the party gaining votes from the previous election; "post-1964" is a dummy variable taking a value of 1 if the election year is 1966 or later, 0 otherwise; standard errors are in parentheses.

TABLE 5.9
Actual and Predicted House Seat Switches to Party Gaining Votes, 1966–1988

Year	Net Seat Gain	Predicted by: 5.8.1	5.8.2	Incumbents Defeated	Predicted by: 5.8.3	5.8.4
1966	47	39	39	39	46	49
1968	5	−4	−13	5	−2	−6
1970	12	15	11	9	12	11
1972	12	7	1	5	8	6
1974	49	59	63	37	41	44
1976	−1	2	−5	7	4	1
1978	15	10	5	14	13	10
1980	34	20	17	27	23	22
1982	26	29	27	22	20	21
1984	14	18	14	13	21	20
1986	5	7	1	5	6	4
1988	−2	−2	−9	2	0	−4
Mean	18	17	13	15	16	15

Note: Estimates based on equations 5.8.2 and 5.8.4 (the third and sixth columns) are computed by applying the 1946–1988 parameters to the 1966–1988 elections.

in light of paltry swings to challengers representing the party gaining votes in these elections.

Observe also that Republicans have done worse than Democrats on this score. In the eight elections since 1966 in which national tides favored Republican House candidates, Republican incumbents added an average of 4.6 percentage points to their vote, while Republican challengers added only 1.4 percentage points; if 1966 is omitted, the mean swing to Republican challengers in these years is a feeble 0.9 percentage points. Swings to Democrats in the four elections favoring them were better balanced—an average swing of 5.2 points to incumbents, 3.3 points to challengers—and both years in which average swings to challengers were greater than average swings to incumbents (1974 and 1982) were "Democratic" years.

In a sense, these findings suggest that incumbency is even more potent a resource than we thought: It protects House members, not by providing wider margins of safety against contrary national tides, but by dampening the tides themselves. But on a deeper level, this finding subverts the whole concept of a swing ratio. The concept (and every method used to estimate it) assumes that some aggregate measure of the House vote reveals the national electorate's partisan preferences and that aggregate vote swings indicate systematic change in these preferences. However, the data in Table 5.7 cast serious doubt on these assumptions. And, indeed, as the electoral politics of Congress have become more district- and candidate-centered and more detached from campaigns for other offices, the notion that aggregate results express anything very meaningful becomes increasingly questionable. When the average vote margin for incumbents of *both* parties increases, as it did in 1968 and 1988, the claim that any aggregate measure represents the national trend provokes skepticism. The same is true when we observe that, as in 1976 or 1986, a party's incumbents enjoy a large average vote gain while its challengers scarcely advance at all. The tidal metaphor no longer seems appropriate.

If the enlarged value of incumbency, as measured in votes, has not really reduced the effects of vote swings on seat swings or deprived Republicans of their rightful share of House seats, the facts remain that House incumbents have been extraordinarily successful in recent elections and that Democrats have easily retained majority control despite Republican dominance in presidential elections. In the present context, the principal explanation for the first fact is that swings to challengers have been much smaller than swings to incumbents of the party favored by national trends (if, indeed, it is meaningful to read "national trends" from any of these results). Remember also that, at least for the 1980s, paltry swings to challengers of the party gaining votes have been associated with weak, inexperienced challengers, particularly among

Republicans. The principal explanation for the second fact is that Republicans have not won enough votes; their aggregate vote has not exceeded 50% by any measure in more than three decades.

THE BIAS OF THE ELECTORAL SYSTEM

Additional grounds for believing that the Republicans' basic problem lies in winning votes rather than in changes in the way votes are translated into seats emerges from an examination of the partisan bias in the electoral system. A simple indicator of partisan bias is the share of seats a party is expected to win if it wins 50% of the vote. An unbiased system would be one in which 50% of the vote was good for 50% of the seats, with symmetrical seat swings for equal vote swings in either direction (King and Gelman 1988). Partisan bias in postwar House elections can thus be estimated by using the parameters from equations in Table 5.5 to compute the expected share of seats won by Democrats when they win 50% of the votes. When this is done, there does appear to be a pro-Democratic bias. According to equation 1 in Table 5.5, with 50% of the total two-party vote for House candidates, the Democrats would have been expected to win 52.1% of the seats between 1946 and 1964, 53.9% between 1966 and 1988. The equivalent estimates from equation 2 are 52.6% and 54.8%, respectively, for the two periods.

But again, these results are distorted by the Democrats' wide lead in uncontested seats. Democrats win a larger share of the seats than their average vote "should" give them because they win a substantial number of seats that do not figure into the mean vote. When equation 2 is rerun with the dependent variable as the Democrats' share of victories *in the seats contested by both parties*—the set from which the independent variable is calculated—we find a strong Republican bias between 1946 and 1964 and almost no bias at all subsequently. With an average of 50% of the votes in these districts, Democrats would have been predicted to win 42.8% of the seats prior to 1966 and 50.6% thereafter.

King and Gelman's (1988) much more complex analysis estimating temporal change in partisan bias leads them to a similar conclusion: The seats-votes relationship in House elections was strongly biased in favor of Republican candidates early in the postwar period; the bias fell to near zero between the 1960s and the early 1980s; and at the very end of the period (1984 and 1986 in their data), a pro-Democratic bias emerged. Taking the effects of incumbency into account, however, they conclude that the electoral system "has remained severely biased toward the Republican party for all elections in the past four decades" (1988:20).

The recent bias in the Democrats' favor is purely an artifact of incumbency (there are more Democratic incumbents).

Clearly, if the underlying seats-votes relationship has consistently favored Republicans, they cannot blame bias in the structure of electoral politics for depriving them of their rightful majorities. Elimination of the bias in their favor may, however, have kept Republicans from winning as many seats as they would have in the past with an equivalent level of popular support. They are worse off because they no longer benefit from a biased electoral system.

GERRYMANDERING

Why has the pro-Republican bias disappeared? A possible reason— and a favorite allegation of Republican officials—is that Democratically controlled state governments have drawn House districts that systematically discriminate against Republican candidates. Flagrant gerrymandering, so the claim goes, protects Democratic incumbents from the electorate's wrath. On this ground, President Bush included among his 1989 campaign reform proposals criteria for redistricting intended to end the practice (Alston and Craney 1989).

In reality, however, Republican difficulties have little to do with gerrymandering. Despite its nefarious reputation, gerrymandering has had surprisingly little systematic impact on congressional elections in the postwar period. The Supreme Court's decision in *Baker* v. *Carr* compelled many states to redraw district lines, occasionally two or three times, during the 1960s. This naturally led to speculation that redistricting might be to blame for the increase in incumbents' vote margins during that decade (Tufte 1973). But further research showed that the incumbency advantage measured by the usual standards was not affected by redistricting; it grew as much in districts that remained unchanged as in those that had been redrawn (Ferejohn 1977; Cover and Mayhew 1981).

Nor has redistricting systematically hurt Republican House candidates. The probit equations in Table 5.10 show that the probability of a Democratic victory is totally unrelated to redistricting. When the previous Democratic vote in the district, the national swing, and incumbency status are taken into account, whether or not district lines were redrawn had no substantively or statistically significant effect on the outcome (equation 1). This remains true when analysis is confined to the period of Republican presidential ascendancy (1968–1988; equation 2). Nor does any significant relationship appear when Republican and Democratic incumbents are analyzed separately.

The only concrete evidence that Republicans have suffered from partisan gerrymandering comes from studies of the 1982 election (Abra-

TABLE 5.10

Probit Estimates of Effects of Redistricting on Partisan Outcomes of House Elections, 1946–1988 and 1968–1988

Variable	1946–1988 (1)	1968–1988 (2)
Intercept	−3.961*** (.169)	−2.668*** (.202)
Vote won by Democratic candidate in last election (%)	.079*** (.003)	.055*** (.004)
National shift in the two-party Democratic vote (%)	.157*** (.007)	.133*** (.012)
Incumbency	.961*** (.039)	1.209*** (.057)
Open seat held by Democrat	−.201* (.097)	−.069 (.126)
District was redrawn	.028 (.061)	−.050 (.084)
Log likelihood	−1,692	−751
Number of cases	7,865	4,052

*$p < .05$, one-tailed test.
***$p < .001$, one-tailed test.

Note: The dependent variable is 1 if a Democrat won the seat, 0 otherwise; "incumbency" is 1 if the Democrat is an incumbent, −1 if the Republican is an incumbent, 0 otherwise; "open seat held by Democrat" is 1 if the election is for an open seat last won by a Democrat, 0 otherwise; "district was redrawn" takes the value of 1 if district lines were redrawn since the last election, 0 otherwise; standard errors are in parentheses.

mowitz 1983; Cain and Campagna 1987). And even here, partisan redistricting cost Republicans a maximum of 3 or 4 seats nationally in an election in which Republicans lost 26 seats (Robertson 1983). Republican officials point to California, where Democrats, in full control of the state government, drew up a plan that, with the help of a strong national swing to the Democrats, enlarged the 22–21 Democratic majority in the state's House delegation to 27–18 (California gained 2 seats from the 1980 census). But this was counterbalanced by Republican efforts elsewhere, notably Indiana, where the Republican state legislature drew district lines intended to turn a 6–5 Democratic advantage to a 4–6 or even 3–7 disadvantage (Indiana lost a district after 1980).

The Indiana gerrymander turned out to be a dismal failure—Democrats currently hold a 7–3 majority in the Indiana House delegation—which tells us something important. Gerrymandering works reliably only to the degree that voters are predictably partisan. As party loyalty has diminished (see Chapter 2), so has the predictability of district electorates.

More fickle electorates, along with numerous constraints imposed by court decisions and political realities (e.g., incumbents are reluctant to give up supporters to enhance their party's overall prospects), make drawing a set of districts that systematically and reliably enhances a party's prospects a formidable technical challenge (Cain 1984). When one party controls the statehouse and legislature, it often tries to accomplish this task (Born 1985), though Bruce Cain and Janet Campagna (1987) found only eleven states where, after 1980, manifestly partisan gerrymanders were imposed.

Even when gerrymandering is achieved, its success tends to be limited (Abramowitz 1983; Born 1985). In California, for example, most of the districts that elected Democrats to the House in the 1980s were not reliably Democratic in other elections. No fewer than 19 of the 27 districts held by Democrats produced pluralities for Ronald Reagan in 1984—and statewide, Reagan was, by congressional standards, a "marginal" winner, taking 58% of the vote. In 1986, the Republican governor George Deukmejian, running for reelection, won 20 of the 27 Democratic House districts (Deukmejian won 62% of the vote statewide). Even in 1982, when Deukmejian won the governorship by an eyelash, he enjoyed pluralities in 5 of the Democratic districts (and his opponent took 1 of the 18 Republican districts). With the right match-up, electorates in all but a small number of California's "Democratic" House districts were perfectly capable of electing Republicans.

CAMPAIGN FINANCE

Gerrymandering cannot explain why Republicans have not won more House seats. Structural bias of this sort has, by the most generous estimate, far too small an effect to account for continued Democratic control. Nor has the campaign finance system that has grown up under the Federal Election Campaign Act of 1973 and its amendments impeded Republican advances, although some Republican leaders believe otherwise (Cook 1989). Republicans have reason to be unhappy with their treatment by campaign contributors—particularly political action committees (PACs)—in the 1986 and 1988 elections, but they mistake cause for effect.

In a large majority of the elections since 1972, Republicans have been more generously financed than Democrats. The data in Figure 5.2 reveal that in every election save 1984 the average Republican incumbent spent more than the average Democratic incumbent. Figure 5.3 shows that, among candidates for open seats, Democrats spent more than Republicans in elections from 1972 through 1978, but Republicans spent more in all five elections since then. And according to the data displayed in Figure

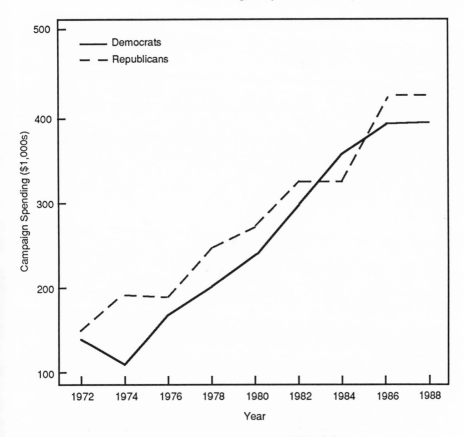

FIGURE 5.2 Campaign Spending by House Incumbents, 1972–1988

5.4, the average Republican challenger outspent the average Democratic challenger in every year but 1974 (for obvious reasons), 1986, and 1988.

It is, of course, the inversion of the advantage illustrated by Figure 5.4 that has suddenly turned Republicans into critics of the campaign finance system. The 1988 election is especially conspicuous when compared to the other years that Republicans took the White House. The average Republican challenger spent 56% more than the average Democratic challenger in 1980, 45% more in 1984, but 31% less in 1988.

Republican party officials are particularly distressed at the way Republican challengers have been treated by political action committees (PACs). It is not difficult to understand why when we observe the trends in the bias of PAC contributors since 1978 shown in Figure 5.5. Bias is computed as the percentage of PAC dollars going to candidates in a category divided by the percentage of candidates who fall into the

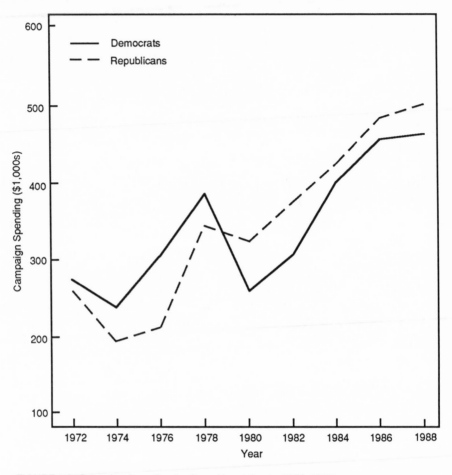

FIGURE 5.3 Campaign Spending for Open House Seats, 1972–1988

category. The more this ratio exceeds 1.0, the greater the bias in favor of candidates in the category; the more it falls short of 1.0, the greater the bias against candidates in the category.

The steepest trends are the growth in the bias for Democratic incumbents and against Republican challengers. Although PACs of all kinds have become increasingly helpful to incumbents and to Democrats (except for labor PACs, who have always favored Democrats overwhelmingly; see Jacobson 1988), Republican officials find the behavior of corporate PACs, presumed to be their ideological allies, the most distressing. In 1980, corporate PACs gave 29% of their contributions to nonincumbent Republican candidates; by 1988, this share had fallen to 6%. Over the same period, the share of corporate PAC money that went

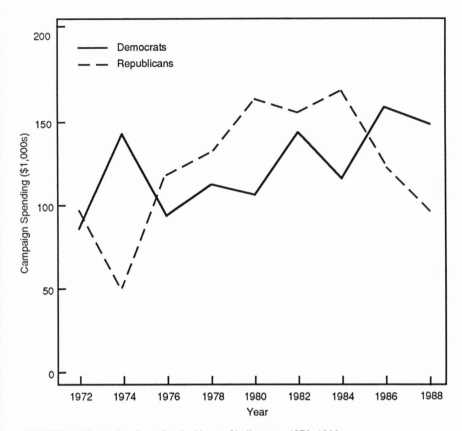

FIGURE 5.4 Campaign Spending by House Challengers, 1972–1988

to Democratic incumbents grew from 36% to 50%. A similar pattern of change is evident among PACs placed in the Federal Election Commission's "trade/membership/health" category. Republican party officials, who once celebrated PACs as the legitimate progeny of a vibrant pluralist democracy, now propose to ban most of them outright (Alston and Craney 1989).

In attacking PACs, however, Republicans are dealing with the effect, not the cause, of their problems. Corporate and trade group PACs did not undergo a conversion to liberalism during the 1980s; rather, they found a dearth of Republican challengers whose prospects were encouraging enough to be worth an investment.[8] Indeed, when the circumstances that affect a candidate's prospects are taken into account, Republican challengers suffered no significant disadvantage over their Democratic counterparts in 1988.

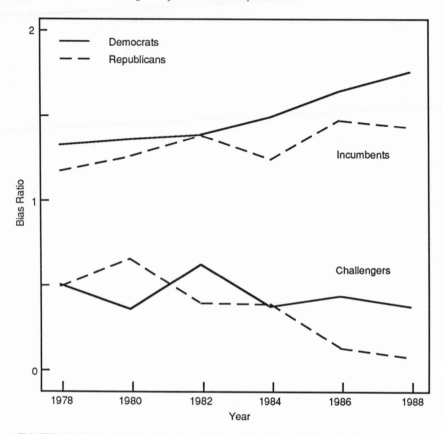

FIGURE 5.5 Bias in PAC Contributions to House Candidates, 1978–1988

We can get a more precise idea of the partisan distribution of campaign money since 1972 by controlling for other circumstances that affect contributions to House candidates. Both the marginality of the seat (how close the incumbent came to losing last time) and the quality of the challenger (whether the challenger has ever held elective office) are known to affect the amounts challengers are able to raise and spend. The coefficients estimated by regressing the challenger's level of spending (adjusted for inflation, 1988 = 1.00) on these variables and the candidate's party in elections from 1972 through 1988 are listed in Table 5.11. A positive coefficient on "party" indicates that Democratic challengers spent more; a negative coefficient indicates that Republican challengers spent more.

The results indicate that only in 1974 and 1986 did Democratic challengers spend significantly more money once marginality and experience are controlled (the coefficient for 1988 is positive, but sub-

TABLE 5.11
Effects of Party and Political Experience on Campaign Spending by House Challengers, 1972–1988

| Year | Regression Coefficient | |
	Party	Previous Experience
1972	−26,280*	70,821***
	(12,781)	(14,176)
1974	85,445***	46,407***
	(11,134)	(12,267)
1976	−75,491***	46,294**
	(13,823)	(14,123)
1978	−79,143***	83,153***
	(17,966)	(21,683)
1980	−91,032***	48,679
	(23,358)	(27,243)
1982	−38,815	82,935**
	(23,874)	(27,271)
1984	−90,346***	144,567***
	(22,537)	(28,547)
1986	51,678*	105,117***
	(22,815)	(30,009)
1988	24,711	123,792***
	(21,326)	(29,011)

*p < .05, one-tailed test.
**p < .01, one-tailed test.
***p < .001, one-tailed test.

Note: Entries are coefficients from regression of the challenger's campaign spending on party (Democrat = 1, Republican = 0), political experience (1 if the candidate has held elective office, 0 otherwise), the vote won by the candidate of the challenger's party in the previous election (%), and a constant; the latter two coefficients are not shown; standard errors are in parentheses.

stantively small and statistically insignificant). Republican challengers were better funded in every election from 1976 through 1984, with only the coefficient for 1982 failing to cross the p < .05 threshold of statistical significance. The Democrats' advantage in 1974 needs no explanation. Although 1986 was also a midterm election in the second term of a Republican president—historically the most promising circumstance for Democratic challengers—the Republicans' deficit here requires some further examination, which will be undertaken in the final chapter. For now, the key message is that, setting 1974 aside, Republican challengers were at a considerable financial advantage until the 1986 election. A similar analysis of incumbent spending (with an additional control for challenger spending, since incumbent spending is demonstrably reactive [Jacobson 1980]) also turned up a Republican advantage in seven of the nine elections, including all three of the cases in which the difference was statistically significant at $p < .05$.

The other coefficient shown in Table 5.11, on previous experience in elective office (that is, my simple measure of quality), shows that in every election save 1980 experienced challengers had significantly more money to spend than did inexperienced challengers. The difference is largest in the three most recent elections. Insofar as Republicans have fielded fewer experienced challengers, this helps to explain why the average Republican challenger has raised less money than the average Democratic challenger in the last two elections. But notice in 1988, when the raw difference is largest (the Democrats spending $143,461, the Republicans $99,383), it shrinks to statistical insignificance once the other variables are taken into account. In other words, once conditions known to influence a challenger's prospects, and thus to guide the strategic decisions of campaign contributors, are taken into account, Republican challengers faced no significant financial bias even in 1988. Their problem was, it again emerges, an unusually weak group of challengers who were, for that reason, ignored by campaign contributors (Cloud 1988).

CONCLUSION

None of the structural explanations for divided government survives analysis. Republican frustration is understandable, but the blame is misplaced. The problem is not that incumbency or gerrymandering have deprived Republicans of their fairly earned share of House seats, but that they have not won enough votes; Republican challengers in particular have continued to fare poorly at the ballot box. The problem is not that the campaign finance system discriminates against Republicans, but that the party has suffered a shortage of challengers with the attributes and electoral prospects that attract contributors. Republican problems are not structural, but political, or so I shall argue in the final chapter.

NOTES

1. In 1946, Democrats held an average of 71% of the state legislative seats in the average House Democrat's state, compared to 25% of the state legislative seats in the average House Republican's state; since then, the difference has diminished to almost nothing; the respective figures for 1988 are 63% and 59%.

2. For a critique of Erikson (1990a), see Jacobson (1990a); see also Erikson's reply (1990b). When the Republican vote in the previous election is substituted for t (time) in Alesina and Rosenthal's version of a model using GNP growth to measure the economy (1989, Table 6), the coefficient on GNP increases from

.07 (with a standard deviation of .16) to .39 (with a standard deviation of .14), and the R^2 increases from .35 to .67. A similar pattern of change occurs in equations using real per capita income growth in place of GNP growth as the measure of the economy's performance.

3. The Gallup Poll data are from King and Ragsdale (1988).

4. Contrary to Erikson's (1990a) results, the coefficient on the economic variable remains substantively large and statistically significant when 1946 is omitted.

5. The chief alternative is the Butler method, named after its author, David Butler, which estimates the swing ratio by examining the hypothetical change in a party's share of seats projected by progressively adding (or subtracting) percentage points to (or from) the actual district vote percentages in a given election (Niemi and Fett 1986). The drawback to this method is that it assumes swings across districts to be uniform, an assumption at increasing odds with reality in House elections (see Chapter 2). Moreover, variations in the swing across districts are no longer random, if they ever were; see the discussion in the text.

6. I also estimated equations allowing for gradual change over time in the swing ratio; the results were not substantively different from those reported here.

7. This latter finding is consistent with my argument that open-seat contests have become more competitive over the postwar period.

8. The reluctance of business PACs to finance Republican challengers was no doubt reinforced by Democratic leaders' blunt reminders of whom it was they would be doing political business with after the election (Jackson 1988).

6

Democratic Hegemony in the House: Political Explanations

The roots of divided government are not structural, but political. The Democrats' continued dominance of the House (as well as of other lower offices) despite Republican presidential victories is a consequence of electoral politics: of candidates, issues, electoral coalitions, and voters' reactions to them. To oversimplify, Republicans have failed to advance in the House because they have fielded inferior candidates on the wrong side of issues that are important to voters in House elections and because voters find it difficult to assign blame or credit when control of the government is divided between the parties. House election outcomes remain responsive to voters' preferences; the demise of representative government has been wildly overstated. Although the connections between voters' preferences and the distribution of House seats have become more contingent, more dependent on candidates and campaigns, than they have been in the past, the low turnover of House seats in the late 1980s does not mean that the distribution of House seats is unresponsive to changes in voters' preferences or that voters' preferences are immune to national forces.

WHAT DO VOTERS WANT?

Voters are, by definition, ultimately responsible for the disjuncture between presidential and congressional election results. A simple political explanation is that Democrats control Congress and Republicans control the White House because voters want it that way. "There is a strong and sensible desire," according to one version of this argument, "in an era when presidential nominating processes give an advantage to extremists or enthusiasts of both parties, to dividing the control of government, for having Tip O'Neill's or Jim Wright's Democrats there to check and balance Ronald Reagan's Republicans" (Barone and Ujifusa 1987:lxii). Morris Fiorina offers a more formal demonstration of the possibility that "some small but important portion of the electorate is engaging in a kind of sophisticated ticket-splitting that permits them to register a preference for a middle course between two parties, neither of which they fully trust to govern" (Fiorina 1988:442).

The spatial logic of Fiorina's argument is compelling, but the initial empirical evidence for it is tenuous, and it requires an uncommon level of strategic sophistication.[1] Fiorina (1990) also outlines an interpretation of ticket splitting that holds that voters divide control because they do not trust politicians of either party; setting the parties at institutional loggerheads lets them foil each other's self-serving schemes. I prefer yet another variant of this approach, one less demanding of voters than ideological balancing—it need not require any conscious calculation at all—and less driven by disenchanted cynicism. Its logic arises from different expectations people have of presidents and congressmen, as well as of Republicans and Democrats, and it emerges from the voters' own self-contradictory policy preferences.

People want mutually exclusive things from government. There is nothing irrational here; we naturally enjoy the benefits government confers but dislike paying for them. As the old saying has it, "Everybody wants to go to heaven, but nobody wants to die." By their nature, budget issues provide the most flagrant examples of incompatible popular demands, but the phenomenon is by no means confined to the budget. Nor is it unique to the 1980s. But in recent years, the electoral expression of contradictory impulses has assumed a form that helps Republican presidential candidates and Democratic House candidates.

Consider the federal budget. Public opinion on budget issues is consistently inconsistent. The idea that budgets should be balanced is so ingrained that more than three-quarters of adult Americans favor a constitutional amendment requiring the federal government to produce one (see Table 6.1). And people leave no doubt about how it should be achieved; more than 80% want to cut spending, fewer than 10% prefer to raise taxes. Even though about half believe that the deficit cannot be reduced without higher taxes, almost two-thirds say they are unwilling to pay more taxes to accomplish this.[2]

If deficits are to be attacked through spending cuts, what should suffer? According to majorities of the public, not health, not education, not Social Security, not student loans, not aid to farmers, not Medicare, not even civil service salaries (see Table 6.2). Indeed, more people believe that spending for the environment, student aid, the unemployed, blacks, Social Security, space research, education, day care, drug eradication, the homeless, and repairing the infrastructure should be increased than believe it should be cut (Table 6.3). More people than not are unwilling to see *any* program they deem worthwhile cut to reduce the

TABLE 6.1
Public Opinion on Balancing the Budget, 1978–1988 (selected years) (percentages)

1. Do you favor or oppose a Constitutional amendment requiring the federal government to balance its budget?

	8/88	11/87	5/87B	9/82[a]	1/79[b]	9/78[b]
Favor	78	75	85	71	73	70
Oppose	10	14	10	20	16	17
Don't know	11	11	6	5	11	13

2. Some people say that the way to reduce the federal budget deficit is to cut back government spending. Others say that the way to do it is to increase taxes. Which solution would you favor— cutting government spending or increasing taxes?

	11/85	2/85	2/84
Cut spending	83	81	82
Increase taxes	7	9	8
Both (volunteered)	7	6	6
Neither (volunteered)	1	2	1
Don't know	2	2	4

3. Do you think that in order to reduce the federal budget deficit substantially, it will be necessary to raise taxes?

	10/88	7/88	1/86	10/84B	10/84A	9/84	8/84
Yes	49	52	46	43	47	43	52
No	43	37	48	47	42	51	38
Don't know	8	11	7	10	11	7	10

4. In order to reduce the size of the federal budget deficit, would you be willing or not to pay more in federal taxes?

	1/88	11/87	1/87	11/85[c]	1/85[c]	1/84[c]	1/83[a]
Willing	36	37	30	36	30	25	38
Not willing	60	60	65	57	66	72	57
Don't know	4	3	5	7	5	4	5

[a]Different wording.
[b]Voters only.
[c]10% more taxes specified.

Source: New York Times/CBS News Poll surveys; see endnote 2.

TABLE 6.2

Public Opinion on Strategies for Reducing the Deficit, 1982–1987 (selected years) (percentages)

1. In order to reduce the federal budget deficit, are you willing or not willing for the government to provide fewer services, even in areas like health and education?

	11/87	9/86[a]
Willing	33	33
Not willing	60	62
Don't know	6	5

2. In order to reduce the size of the federal budget deficit would you be willing to have the government reduce scheduled cost-of-living adjustments for people who receive Social Security?

	11/87	1/85	1/83	5/82	3/82
Willing	22	23	42	31	37
Not willing	73	73	53	61	57
Don't know	5	3	5	8	6

3. It is expected that if Ronald Reagan's budget for next year is adopted, the federal government could spend as much as $200 billion more than it takes in. To reduce the size of the federal budget deficit, would you be willing or not willing to

	5/87		
	Willing	Not willing	Don't know
a. Reduce the amount of money available for student loans?	33	60	6
b. Reduce aid to farmers?	27	68	5
c. Reduce proposed spending on military and defense programs?	54	40	6
d. Postpone tax cuts for people earning $50,000 or more?	49	43	7

4. In order to reduce the size of the federal budget deficit, do you think it would be a good idea for the government to spend less on programs to (1) help farmers, (2) Medicare, (3) Amtrak, (4) cut salaries of all federal civil service employees or would that be a bad idea?

	1/85			
	Farmers	Medicare	Amtrak	Civil service
Good idea	27	18	50	38
Bad idea	65	77	36	50
Don't know	8	5	14	12

[a]Different wording.

Source: New York Times/CBS News Poll surveys; see endnote 2.

TABLE 6.3
Public Opinion on Spending for Government Programs, 1986 and 1988 (percentages)

1. If you had a say in making up the federal budget this year, for which of the following programs
   would you like to see spending increased and for which would you like to see spending decreased?
   Should federal spending on _____ be increased, decreased, or kept about the same?

	Increased	Decreased	Same	Don't know
1986				
Improving and protecting the environment	48	4	44	4
Aid for college students	39	12	45	4
Social Security	63	3	31	2
Food stamps	23	29	40	8
Aid to the Contras	8	58	19	15
Assistance to the unemployed	38	13	45	4
Space and scientific research	31	23	41	5
Programs that assist blacks	25	16	52	6
1988				
Education programs	71	3	21	4
Day care and after-school care for children	52	10	30	8
Combatting illegal drugs	75	6	14	5
Helping the homeless	68	4	23	5
Repairing and maintaining highways and bridges	39	6	52	3

2. One reason government spending is so high is that everyone fights for the programs they think are
   worthwhile. Is there a government program which you think is worthwhile that you would be willing
   to see cut in order to reduce the deficit?

	1/85
Yes	31
No	45
Don't know	24

*Source: New York Times/CBS News Poll surveys (the "1988" section of question 1 [7/88] and question
2); 1986 American National Election Study (the "1986" section of question 1); see endnote 2.*

deficit. The only cuts that win majority approval are of defense programs
(at least after the enormous buildup of the early 1980s), most particularly
aid to the Contras, food stamps, and Amtrak. A narrow majority is also
willing to postpone tax reductions for people earning $50,000 or more.

Similarly contradictory desires appear in other contexts as well. More
people think business is over-regulated than think it under-regulated,
but two-thirds agree that "protecting the environment is so important
that requirements and standards cannot be too high and continuing
environmental improvements must be made regardless of cost" (Table
6.4). Large majorities also think the government should guarantee
employment to all who want to work, medical care for everyone, and
day care and after-school care for children. Americans clearly dislike
intrusive, expensive "big government"; they also clearly appreciate most
of the programs that comprise it and want more of them.

TABLE 6.4

Public Opinion on Government Activities, 1981–1988 (selected years) (percentages)

1. Do you think the federal government regulates business too much these days, does it regulate business too little, or does it impose the right amount of regulation on business?

	1/86
Too much	41
Too little	22
Right amount	22
Depends	2
Don't know	13

2. Do you agree or disagree with the following statement? Protecting the environment is so important that requirements and standards cannot be too high and continuing environmental improvements must be made regardless of cost.

	7/88	1/86	4/83	9/82	9/81
Agree	66	66	58	52	45
Disagree	22	27	34	41	42
Don't know	12	7	8	7	13

3. I'd like to know what you think the responsibilities of the federal government are. For each of these items, please tell me if you think this is something the government in Washington should or should not be doing.

	11/87		
	Should	Should not	Don't know
a. Regulating airline prices and schedules	38	55	7
b. Upholding traditional moral values	53	41	7
c. Seeing to it that everyone who wants a job, has a job	71	26	3
d. Guaranteeing medical care for all people	78	19	3
e. Seeing to it that day care and after-school care for children are available	62	35	3
f. Supporting anti-communist forces around the world	52	41	8

Source: New York Times/CBS News Poll surveys; see endnote 2.

This creates a politically significant variation on the classic collective goods problem. Technically, a collective good is one that everyone shares because it cannot, by its nature, be provided exclusively to any individual or subset of individuals; if anyone enjoys the good, everyone does. The most common political example is national defense, but there are many others. The problem arises because collective goods, by definition, cannot be withheld from people who do not contribute to their production. That makes it economically rational for any individual to avoid, if possible, paying her or his share—to be, in the jargon, a free rider. Since this is true for every individual, collective goods will not be provided (or, more realistically, will be provided at grossly suboptimal levels) absent some institutional arrangement for assuring that the costs be paid.[3] It makes no sense to contribute to producing a collective good even if the value of the good to you outweighs its cost to you unless you can depend on others to contribute as well, and if logic recommends free riding, there is no reason to expect others to contribute and so no reason to contribute yourself.

Solving such problems is a central purpose of government, to which we grant a monopoly on the legitimate use of coercion so it can, among other things, produce collective goods. It is perfectly rational for an individual to support the creation of an Internal Revenue Service, backed by courts and jails, that taxes him to pay for collective goods because such institutional arrangements guarantee that others will have to pay, too, and that the collective goods can therefore be purchased. It is also perfectly rational for the same individual to hire the best tax lobbyist and best tax attorney he can afford in order to minimize his own share of the taxes.

An analogous logic applies to contemporary political issues. Majorities plainly, and understandably, desire some broad collective goods: low taxes, a balanced budget, low inflation, less intrusive government, adequate national defense. Aside from defense, all of these goods presumably contribute to economic efficiency, itself a quintessential collective good, and hence to another, economic growth. But just as understandably, majorities prefer to avoid the costs required to secure these collective goods: cuts in government programs and benefits, higher unemployment, greater exposure to market forces, greater environmental risk. These costs are more narrowly focused, and they outweigh the benefits of the broader collective goods to those who get stuck with them. People rationally prefer a job to lower inflation, a larger Social Security check or even a local sewage treatment facility to an imperceptibly smaller deficit. No one has an incentive to sacrifice income or local benefits to greater economic efficiency, or even to risk such a sacrifice if the risk is appreciable.

In the past decade or so, the parties have taken positions that allow voters to express both sets of preferences at the polls: They can vote for Republican presidential candidates committed to the diffuse collective goods of low taxes, economic efficiency, and a strong national defense, and for congressional Democrats who promise to minimize the price they have to pay for these goods in forgone benefits.

EXPECTATIONS OF PARTIES AND INSTITUTIONS

The ground for this sort of ticket splitting is evident in the way the public views the strengths of the two parties. During the 1980s, Republicans have been judged better than Democrats at ensuring prosperity, handling inflation, reducing the deficit (at least until 1988), maintaining a strong defense, and, since late 1984, keeping us out of war (Table 6.5). Democrats have been thought better at handling unemployment, protecting Social Security, dealing with farm problems, handling the problem of toxic wastes, improving education, and helping the poor and the middle class. Democrats are also considered more likely to create a fair budget and tax system and are considered more attentive to groups stuck with the bill for the collective benefits of greater economic efficiency and growth: women, union members, farmers, blacks, and "people like you." Republicans are thought to be more solicitous only of "big business" and "the rich" (Table 6.6).

Perceived differences between the parties coincide with differences in what people expect of presidents and members of Congress, which in turn reflect differences in the political incentives created by their respective institutional positions. Presidents are supposed to pursue broad national interests; uniquely among elected officials, presidents can profit politically by producing diffuse collective benefits at the expense of concentrated particular interests.

Members of Congress, in contrast, survive by looking out for the particular, because this is what voters want from them. When it comes to congressional representation, most people prefer "delegates" who put district preferences ahead of the national interest to "trustees" who invert these priorities (Table 6.7); helping people in the district is a more important part of the job than working on national legislation. Moreover, most believe that members of Congress *are* more concerned with local than with Washington opinion, overwhelmingly so when specific reference is made to the respondent's own representative.

This combination of partisan and institutional expectations clearly strengthens Republican presidential candidates, particularly when they are given superior marks for personal competence, which presumably contributes to their ability to deliver desired collective benefits. It also

TABLE 6.5

Public Opinion on Parties' Ability to Handle Problems, 1981–1988 (selected years) (percentages)

1. Regardless of how you usually vote, do you think the Republican party or the Democratic party . . .

	Rep.	Dem.	Both	Neither	Don't know
a. Is more likely to keep us out of war?					
10/88[a]	40	30	3	5	20
9/86[a]	40	31	4	6	18
10/84A[a]	37	34	3	6	20
10/82[c]	33	34	7	8	18
9/82[c]	35	39	3	5	17
4/81[c]	29	37	2	13	19
b. Is more likely to make sure the country is prosperous?					
9/86[a]	45	35	5	4	12
c. Is better able to ensure a strong economy?					
10/88[a]	51	31	2	4	12
10/84A[a]	54	27	2	4	13
d. Is better able to handle inflation?					
12/85	50	26	3	7	15
6/83[c]	41	32	4	6	17
10/82[c]	46	32	3	6	13
9/82[c]	38	33	3	10	15
5/82[c]	35	34	3	10	18
4/81[c]	45	17	0	24	14
e. Is more likely to reduce the federal budget deficit?					
8/88[c]	30	41	1	12	15
12/85	45	28	4	10	14
6/85[b]	45	25	0	13	17
10/84A	43	30	1	10	16
5/82[b]	46	28	3	7	16
f. Is better able to handle unemployment?					
9/86[a]	37	40	3	6	13
12/85	36	40	3	7	14
10/84A[a]	44	37	2	3	14
6/83[c]	30	48	3	6	12
10/82[a]	30	52	3	4	12
5/82[c]	23	51	3	7	17
4/81[c]	36	31	4	11	18

continues

Table 6.5 (*continued*)

	Rep.	Dem.	Both	Neither	Don't know
g. Is better at keeping the Social Security system healthy?					
9/86[a]	33	46	5	7	10
10/84A[b]	24	54	5	3	13
h. Is likely to make the right decisions about Social Security?					
10/82[a]	30	49	4	4	14
9/82[c]	27	54	3	4	12
5/82[c]	27	52	3	4	12
i. Is more likely to create a budget that is fair to all people?					
12/85	32	40	5	7	16
10/82[c]	35	45	3	6	12
9/82[c]	32	50	2	5	11
5/82[c]	28	46	4	7	16
j. Would do a better job of solving the problems faced by American farmers?					
9/86[a]	23	52	2	6	17
2/86[b]	17	42	6	7	28
12/85	18	54	5	10	14
k. Cares about the needs and problems of people like yourself?					
9/86[a]	26	52	6	4	11
4/86[b]	34	44	6	7	10
12/85[b]	31	42	6	11	10
10/84[ab]	36	46	4	3	11
5/82[b]	28	51	4	6	11
l. Is better at protecting the environment?					
10/88[a]	28	42	4	5	20

[a]Probable voters.
[b]Different wording.
[c]Registered voters.

Source: New York Times/CBS News Poll surveys; see endnote 2.

TABLE 6.6
Public Opinion on Parties' Concerns, 1985 (percentages)

1. Who do you think cares more about the needs and problems of _____ , the Republican party or the Democratic party?

| | 12/85 | | | | |
	Rep.	Dem.	Both	Neither	Don't know
Big business	66	17	5	2	11
Women	22	48	7	6	17
Union members	17	63	3	2	15
Farmers	18	54	5	10	14
Blacks	16	57	8	5	15
People like you	31	42	6	11	10

2. Who do you think is more concerned about seeing that the tax system is fair—the Republicans in Congress or the Democrats in Congress?

	6/85
Republicans	35
Democrats	40
Both	7
Neither	4
Don't know	14

Source: New York Times/CBS News Poll surveys; see endnote 2.

helps congressional Democrats, because people want representatives who will protect them from damaging policies regardless of the policies' broader benefits. Voters thus use quite different criteria for judging presidential and congressional candidates. Presidential candidates are evaluated according to their views on national issues and their competence in dealing with national problems (Table 6.8; see also Popkin et al. 1976; Kiewiet and Rivers 1985). Congressional candidates are evaluated on their personal character and experience and on their devotion to district services and local issues (Jacobson 1987b).

An interesting consequence of the distinction voters draw between presidents and members of Congress is that large majorities want Congress, rather than the president, to determine where cuts should be made to balance the budget (Table 6.9). Survey respondents say they prefer Congress to make the decisions because is it is more decentralized, permeable, and responsive to the public than is the White House. In other words, Congress has to pay much more attention to the question of who will bear the concentrated costs of producing the diffuse collective benefits of a balanced budget. People have few illusions about the consequences; few expect the five-year timetable for reaching a balanced budget under Gramm-Rudman-Hollings to be met, and most think

116

TABLE 6.7
Public Opinion on Role of Members of Congress, 1978, 1986, and 1987 (percentages)

1. If a member of Congress thinks a bill is in the best interest of the country, but a majority of the people he or she represents are against it, should the member of Congress vote for the bill or vote against it?

	5/87B
For	34
Against	59
Depends	3
Don't know	4

2. What do you think is a more important way for a Congressman to spend his time—helping people in his district who have problems with the government, or working in Congress on bills of national interest?

	9/78
Helping people in his district	48
Working on national bills	28
Both	21
Don't know	3

3. Would you say that most members of Congress are more concerned about what people in Washington, D.C. think or more concerned about what people in the districts they represent think? (probable voters only)

	10/86
People in Washington	38
People in districts	49
Both	4
Neither	1
Don't know	8

4. What about the member of the House of Representatives from your district? Is that representative more concerned about what people in Washington, D.C. think or more concerned about what people in your district think?

	10/86
People in Washington	20
People in districts	64
Both	3
Neither	1
Don't know	11

Source: New York Times/CBS News Poll surveys; see endnote 2.

TABLE 6.8
Public Opinion on Criteria for Voting in Presidential and Congressional Elections, 1982, 1986, and 1987 (percentages)

1. Some people choose among presidential candidates by picking the one closest to them on important issues. Some other people choose the one who has the personal characteristics—like integrity or leadership—they want most in a president. Which is more important when *you* choose—issues or personal characteristics?

	10/87
Issues	54
Personal characteristics	34
Both	8
Neither, don't know	4

2. Sometimes people decide to vote for a candidate for the U.S. House of Representatives because of national issues. Sometimes it's because of local or state issues. Sometimes it's because of the candidate's political party. And sometimes it's because of the candidate's character or experience. This year, what will make the biggest difference in how you vote—a national issue, a local or state issue, the candidate's political party, or the candidate's character or experience? (probable voters only)

	10/86	9/86	4/86[a]
National	22	20	30
State and local	25	23	20
Party	6	9	1
Character/experience	40	41	37
Other/don't know	7	7	11

3. Would you be more likely to vote for a candidate for the U.S. House who is more interested in helping people in your district who have a problem with the government, or for a candidate who is more interested in working in Congress on bills of *national* interest? (probable voters only)

	9/86	10/82
District	47	54
National	40	36
Both	8	5
Don't know	4	5

[a]Different wording.

Source: New York Times/CBS News Poll surveys; see endnote 2.

TABLE 6.9
Public Opinion on Institutional Responsibility for the Budget, 1982, 1985, and 1986 (percentages)

1. Last year the president and Congress agreed to a law requiring the federal budget to be balanced within the next five years. Who do you think would make better decisions about what to do to reduce the federal deficit, Ronald Reagan or Congress?

	1/86
Reagan	29
Congress	59
Both equal	4
Neither	2
Don't know	6

2. Who *should* have the most say about what cuts should be made to balance the budget—the president or Congress?

	11/85
President	20
Congress	71
Both equal	4
Don't know	5

What is the main reason you feel that way? (those answering "Congress")

More people have input	26
Power not concentrated in one person	10
Representativeness, for the people	16
Other	13

3. In your opinion, whose responsibility for balancing the budget is greater, the president's or that of Congress?

	1/82
President	23
Congress	63
Both equal	9
Don't know	5

4. Do you think the budget will be balanced within five years?

	1/86
Yes	15
No	77
Don't know	8

If not, whose fault will that be, the president's or Congress'?

President	15
Congress	35
Both	20
Don't know	7

Source: New York Times/CBS News Poll surveys; see endnote 2.

TABLE 6.10
Public Opinion on Divided Control of Federal Government, 1981 and 1989 (percentages)

1. Do you think it is better for the country to have a president who comes from the same political party that controls Congress, or do you think it is better to have a president from one political party and Congress controlled by another?

	9/89	11/81
Same party	35	47
Different parties	45	34
Don't know	20	19

Source: New York Times/CBS News Poll surveys; see endnote 2.

Congress will be more to blame than the president. Still, people prefer Congress to control the decisions.

Ironically, these attitudes may benefit both Republican presidents and congressional Democrats and thus contribute to the maintenance of divided government. Republican presidents can claim credit for pursuing a balanced budget but are absolved in advance of blame for failing. The blame falls on Congress, but its members are notoriously skilled at avoiding individual responsibility for their collective decisions, and they profit individually from fighting to protect local interests and benefits (Mayhew 1974a; Fenno 1978). When neither side suffers politically from the deficit, no one has much incentive to impose painful spending cuts or tax increases to reduce it; the public is wise to be skeptical.

By this argument, then, it is not so much that voters balance Democrats in one branch against Republicans in the other to get a government closer to their centrist views, but that majorities prefer a president committed to a set of diffuse collective goods and congressional representatives committed to minimizing what they have to give up to achieve those collective goods. This requires neither egregious cynicism nor even conscious calculation on the part of voters. Offered two presidential candidates, voters choose the one they think more likely to keep taxes low and defense strong and to govern competently. Offered two House candidates, voters choose the one they think more likely to deliver local benefits and to protect their favorite programs. Voters need not even recognize that the goals are interdependent.

Cast in this form, the hypothesis that divided government reflects voters' preferences makes a good deal of sense. But whatever its source, Americans have grown increasingly content with divided control of the federal government (Table 6.10), perhaps because the standoff has kept taxes down and spending on popular programs up. The resulting budget deficits have so far brought little palpable pain, and some respectable economists argue that they never will. Until divided control can be plausibly blamed for some policy disaster, budgetary or otherwise, or partisanship becomes more intense and widespread, voters have little reason to be unhappy about divided government.

IDEOLOGY AND THE QUALITY OF CANDIDATES

The stylized account of congressional activity outlined in the previous section also points to one reason Republicans have found it more difficult to field attractive congressional challengers than might be expected of an ascendant party. The view of government that serves Republican presidential candidates well clashes with the realities of what it takes to win and hold seats in Congress. For the most part, congressional careers are built on delivering particularized benefits to constituents, not on dismantling, in the name of efficiency and economy, programs that create the benefits. Members are elected to minimize the local cost of producing national collective goods, not to pursue visions of the national interest regardless of local consequences. Thus people embracing the minimalist conception of government underlying the "Reagan revolution" are unlikely to find a congressional career enticing or, once initiated, satisfying. If government is the problem, not the solution, why pursue a career in politics that can only succeed if you are willing to become part of the problem? Those Republicans most strongly attracted to the party's conservative ideology are, by that very fact, ill suited to the politics of congressional elections.

The view of government held by most Democrats is, in contrast, far more positive. Their traditions and ideas sanction government assistance to all sorts of groups for all sorts of purposes. Democrats can still believe that government is an honorable calling and that the activities sustaining a congressional career are worthwhile. Democrats thus have far less trouble fielding attractive, experienced challengers comfortable with the demands of contemporary electoral politics and keeping them happy once they have reached the House.

The conflict Republican legislators face is illustrated by the experience of the House Republicans who first took office along with Ronald Reagan in 1980. The Republican class of 1980 was outstanding for its inexperience, ideological rigidity, and loyalty to Reagan's agenda. In their commitment to reversing fifty years of government growth, some of its members disdained to spare federal programs that were the lifeblood of their districts. One of them, John Hiler of Indiana, put it this way: "My solution is to cut down on the tax money flowing from South Bend to Washington rather than to increase the grant money flowing from Washington to South Bend" (Hook 1988:2663).

TABLE 6.11
Voluntary Retirements from the House, 1981–1989

	Democrats	Republicans
Retired	24 (2.4)*	29 (4.1)
Ran for another office	36 (3.6)	34 (4.8)
Total	60 (5.9)*	63 (8.9)
Number of incumbents	1,012	710

*Party difference in percentages is significant at $p < .05$.

Note: Percentage of incumbents in the category is in parentheses.

After heady victories in 1981 on budget and tax cuts, political reality, in the form of the 1982 election, intruded. Half the Republican incumbents who lost in 1982 were freshmen, the largest proportion since 1966; 25% of the Republican class of 1980 were denied a second term. Those who remained learned to appreciate the political value of defending local interests and providing particularized benefits to constituents. Hiler, for example, "continued to advocate the abolition of such programs as Urban Development Action Grants, but he also made sure South Bend got its share so long as the programs survived" (Hook 1988:2264). Others began to pay more attention to constituents' problems and district needs. As one of them, Dan Coats of Indiana, eventually concluded, "It's nice to talk about eliminating government, until people realized that eliminating it affected their lives" (Hook 1988:2265).

Not all adapted, to be sure. By the beginning of the 101st Congress in 1989, only thirty of the fifty-two members of the Republican class of 1980 remained in office; in addition to the thirteen defeated for reelection, nine sought higher office or retired outright. The rate of voluntary departure of this class—17%—exceeds that of other Republican incumbents, not to mention Democrats. On the whole, Republicans have been significantly more likely than Democrats to depart the House voluntarily during the Reagan-Bush years. Table 6.11 reveals that from 1981 through 1989, more Republicans (sixty-three) than Democrats (sixty) have departed the House voluntarily even though there were many more Democratic incumbents. In percentage terms, 5.9% of the incumbent Democrats who could have run for reelection chose not to, compared to 8.9% of the Republicans; the difference is significant at $p < .05$. The party difference in "pure" retirements—those not accepting or seeking another public office—is also statistically significant.

Although minority status is an obvious source of frustration, it cannot by itself account for these differences. John Hibbing (1982) found that, between 1959 and 1978, Republicans were, other things equal, *less* likely than Democrats to retire voluntarily. Their minority status was at least as firm in the 1960s and 1970s as it was in the 1980s; indeed, after the 1980 election, Republican prospects for achieving majority status appeared better than they had in years. Although the evidence of this sort is admittedly circumstantial, it is consistent with the idea that the activities that comprise and sustain a congressional career are, other things equal, more congenial, at present, to Democrats than to Republicans.[4]

TIMING

Whatever deleterious effects the contemporary job description might have had on the quality of Republican House challengers may well have been compounded by the peculiar incidence of electoral tides in the 1980s. Several of the patterns observed in Chapter 4—the concentration of competition into fewer House seats, the recent falloff in the quality of challengers and in funds for their campaigns—imply that career and contribution strategies are shaped by long-term as well as short-term expectations. The fewer incumbents defeated or even threatened with defeat, the more reluctant good candidates are to run and contributors are to support challengers. And insofar as career and contribution decisions are shaped retrospectively, the elections of the 1980s can only have discouraged potential Republican House candidates and their potential supporters.

The 1982 election was the critical turning point. The Republican party had triumphed in 1980, taking the White House, the Senate, and picking up an additional 34 seats in the House to reach their highest total since Watergate; 26 more seats would give them a majority. A sense of momentum and the administration's successes in 1981 helped Republicans to recruit a decent crop of challengers for 1982. But by election day, the economy was in deep recession, unemployment had reached double digits, and popular dissatisfaction with Reagan was at the highest point of his entire presidency. Only one Republican challenger was successful (though the threat of formidable Republican challenges probably helped save some Republican incumbents by reducing funds available to the strong crop of Democratic challengers; see Jacobson 1985–1986).

The nearly total futility of Republican challenges in 1982 probably hampered Republican recruitment for 1984. The party had, in effect, used up some of its most promising talent in the wrong election. Thus few effective Republican challengers were poised to take advantage of Reagan's landslide victory, and whatever opportunity it may have presented was largely missed (Jacobson 1985a). Republicans gained only 14 House seats. This experience made it more difficult to attract high-quality Republican challengers for 1986. Democratic incumbents who had survived the Reagan landslide would be tougher to defeat without

Reagan to head the ticket, and the historic record for the president's party at the midterm election six years into an administration was dismal. The aggregate result was that the 1986 Republican challengers were nearly as inexperienced and neglected by campaign contributors as were the 1988 contingent.

Ironically, election day 1986 found the economy still growing nicely and Reagan's performance receiving widespread popular approval. And survey evidence suggests that approval of Reagan and optimism about the economy translated into votes for Republican House candidates—especially when combined with strong challenges. Republicans might have done considerably better in 1986 had they fielded a group of challengers as talented as those who ran in 1982 (Jacobson and Kernell 1990). The same might be said of 1988; but in 1988, Republicans acted as if they had given up hope of making any progress in the House, which guaranteed that they did not. In short, congressional Republicans suffered from bad timing in the 1980s.

NATIONAL FORCES IN THE 1980s

This interpretation rests on the assumption that national conditions—the economy, presidential politics, political issues, Republican gains among party identifiers—were conducive to Republican success in the three most recent elections, but Republican candidacies were too feeble to exploit the opportunities proffered. An alternative view is that conditions in fact offered Republican challengers little leverage against congressional Democrats, and so potential Republican challengers and contributors acted quite rationally when they stayed on the sidelines after 1982.

The conjunction of three circumstances is required to defeat congressional incumbents: a good candidate, a good reason for voters to desert the incumbent, and enough money to acquaint voters with both (Jacobson 1987b; Iyengar and Kinder 1987). All are necessary, none is sufficient by itself, and all are related. Good candidates attract money, and the promise of money attracts good candidates. But both depend on the likelihood of winning, which depends, in turn, on the availability of issues and arguments that might erode the incumbent's support. Without exploitable issues, even experienced, well-financed challengers can expect to make little headway (just as vulnerable incumbents win easy reelection if they escape a challenger with the skill and resources to exploit their vulnerabilities). Thus if potential Republican challengers could turn up no telling issues during the Reagan-Bush years, sitting tight was a rational strategy.

From this perspective, the very success of Republican presidents left Republican challengers with little leverage against Democratic incum-

TABLE 6.12
House Seat Swings Between Presidential Elections, 1932–1988

Presidential Success	House Seat Swing to or from President's Party
President's party relinquished White House	
1932*	−150
1952	−50
1960*	−28
1968	−52
1976*	−50
1980	−49
President's party retained White House with reduced vote	
1940	−66
1944	−24
1948*	20
1988*	−7
President reelected with increased vote	
1936	20
1956*	−20
1964	33
1972*	0
1984*	−10

*Elections held in circumstances of divided party control (at least one house of Congress controlled by the other party at the time of the election).

Note: The seat swing is measured from presidential election year to presidential election year.

bents. Divided control of the federal government divides responsibility for success or failure as well. If the public mood is positive, if peace and prosperity reign, incumbents of both parties can claim a share of the credit. A campaign for reelection (or to elect a sitting vice president) promoting themes of affirmation and continuity gives the congressional challengers of the president's party little rhetorical ammunition. It is hard to make a case for throwing the rascals in Congress out while telling voters, "don't worry, be happy."

The historical pattern of electoral swings since the New Deal realignment bears out this intuition. Table 6.12 shows how partisan representation in the House has changed under three levels of presidential success. The difference in House seats is measured from the previous presidential election, not from the immediately preceding midterm, because I am concerned here with changes over the course of the entire administration; the relative contribution of the midterm and presidential election to the total is beside this point. Elections held in circumstances of divided party control (at least one house of Congress controlled by the other party at the time of the election) are marked with an asterisk.

Failed presidencies—those followed by a switch in party control—invariably cost the president's party a substantial number of House seats, and this happens regardless of whether the president's party also controls the House. When a party has relinquished the White House in the postwar era, it has won, on average, 46 fewer House seats than it had won in the previous presidential election year. When a party has retained the presidency, but with a smaller share of the vote than before, it has also lost House seats—with the notable exception of the Democrats in 1948.

The most successful presidencies have produced additional House seats for the president's party under unified control, but not under divided party control. The landslide reelections of Franklin D. Roosevelt in 1936 and Lyndon Johnson in 1964 raised Democratic House majorities above the levels reached in the previous presidential election. The Republican landslides of 1956, 1972, and 1984, however, left the Republicans with the same number or fewer House seats than they had won when the Republican president was first elected.

Of the five elections held under circumstances of divided party control in which the president's party retained the White House, only 1948 left the president's party stronger in the House than it had been four years earlier. The 1948 election was also the only one of this set held amidst widespread public discontent and the only one that did not feature a highly personalized, "feel-good" presidential campaign. Truman was able to saddle the Republican Congress with blame for inflation and economic difficulties (strikes, dislocations produced by the transition to a peacetime economy) as well as for threatening popular New Deal programs, and congressional Democrats were the beneficiaries.

In historical perspective, then, the Republicans' inability to match or exceed the 192 House seats they won in 1980 in any of the subsequent four elections is not so surprising. The recession of 1982 hurt, as midterm recessions always do. But the years of prosperity that followed the recession, while contributing strongly to victories by Reagan in 1984 and Bush in 1988, did not leave Republican congressional challengers with persuasive arguments that could be used to unseat Democratic incumbents.

The Reagan administration repeated a familiar pattern. The economy has been in recession in five of the six postwar midterm elections held during Republican administrations (1986 is the exception), and Republican congressional candidates have suffered the consequences. But the economy has always rebounded strongly by the time of the presidential election (the GNP growing by an average of 5.3%, with a low of 3.9% for the election year, compared to an average growth rate of -0.5% for the preceding midterm year). Republican presidential candidates have benefitted from the timing of the business cycle, but not in a context where the benefits could extend to Republican congressional challengers. *Their* largest gains have occurred under Democratic administrations.

I do not wish to make too much of this argument. The available observations do not distinguish clearly between outcomes deriving from divided control and simple partisan differences (e.g., all of the highly successful presidencies occurring under divided control were Republican; those occurring under unified control were Democratic). The point remains, however, that the logic of retrospective voting (Fiorina 1981a), applied in circumstances of divided control, does not offer much encouragement to Republican challengers when Republican administrations produce good times, while it continues to promise punishment when administrations fail to do so.

PARTY IDENTIFICATION

Aside from their string of presidential victories, the other principal reason for expecting Republicans to be winning more congressional seats (and other lower offices) is that the electorate has become decidedly more Republican over the last decade. This is shown by Figure 6.1, which traces the percentage of Republicans among party identifiers (including those leaning toward a party) in the American National Election Studies (ANES) from 1952 through 1988. A similar change is registered in other polls (Jacobson 1990c; MacKuen, Erikson, and Stimson 1989).[5] A larger proportion of Republicans turn out to vote—the distribution of party identification among self-reported voters is typically 3 or 4 percentage points more Republican than it is among all ANES respondents—so by 1988 the electorate had become equally divided between Republicans and Democrats.

Republican euphoria and Democratic despair ought to be tempered, however, by signs that this change portends rather less than traditional interpretations of party identification would have it. First, notice the sawtooth pattern in Figure 6.1, which indicates that more people think of themselves as Republicans in presidential election years than at the midterm; the single exception is 1964, which is also the only postwar election in which the Democrats won more than 50.1% of the total votes cast or in which the balance of partisan defections favored the Democrats. The aggregate distribution of party identifiers thus reflects, in part, the electorate's presidential leanings. It also reflects the electorate's choice in House elections; the regression equation in Table 6.13 shows that changes in the distribution of party identification track with House seat swings as well as with presidential voting. Evidently, a noticeable portion of the citizenry responds to questions about partisanship in

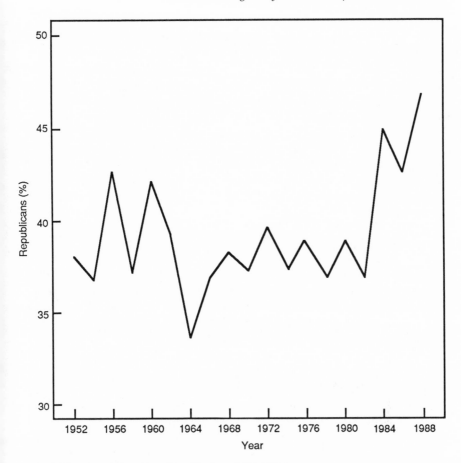

FIGURE 6.1 Republican Party Identification, 1952–1988

terms of their current vote intention. At least at the margins, then, party identification is endogenous; it is moved by the same short-term forces that produce electoral swings.

Second, the distribution of party identification has become less stable and more responsive to short-term factors, including the president's standing with the public, during the Reagan-Bush years (Fiorina 1988; Jacobson 1990c). The responsiveness of "macropartisanship"—the aggregate distribution of party identifiers—to citizens' views of the economy and the president on a monthly basis during the postwar era has been carefully documented by Michael MacKuen, Robert Erikson, and James Stimson (1989). Two additional findings from their research are relevant to our discussion. First, variance in macropartisanship has increased since the 1970s. Second, their model predicts the more volatile swings

TABLE 6.13

Change in Macropartisanship as Function of Election Results for President and House, 1952–1988

Variables	(1)
Intercept	−17.63**
	(5.49)
Seat swing to Democrats (%)	.23*
	(.10)
Democratic presidential vote (%)	.32**
	(.11)
Midterm election	18.88***
	(5.63)
Adjusted R²	.70
Durbin-Watson	2.59
Number of cases	18

*p < .05, one-tailed test.
**p < .01, one-tailed test.
***p < .001, one-tailed test.

Note: The dependent variable is the percentage of all party identifiers, including leaners, who call themselves Democrats. "Seat swing to Democrats" is the change in the percentage of seats held by Democrats from the last election. "Democratic presidential vote" is the percentage of the two-party vote won by the Democratic presidential candidate; it takes the value of 0 at midterms. "Midterm election" takes the value of 1 for midterm elections, 0 otherwise. Standard errors are in parentheses.

in party identification of the recent period as well as it did the more subdued swings of the earlier period; the explanatory power of their equation is greatest for the 1979–1988 period (adjusted $R^2 = .82$, compared to .61 or lower for earlier periods).[6]

When we combine this evidence with the observation (Chapter 2, Figure 2.3) that party loyalty among presidential voters was higher in 1984 and 1988 than in any election since the National Election Studies were initiated in 1952, while loyalty among House and Senate voters remained at the lower levels of the last two decades, the obvious implication is that there is less substance behind the growth in Republican party identification than conventional notions of "partisan realignment" would suggest. To the degree that Republican gains simply reflect the success of their presidential candidates in an era when shallow party attachments free more people to respond to questions about partisanship in terms of their current presidential preference or opinion of the president, then it is not so surprising that the shift has had little visible consequence in elections for other offices. As Martin Wattenberg (1990) has pointed out, partisan habits used to be *stronger* in elections for lower offices, presumably because party cues faced less competition from conflicting bits of information. That they are now weaker supports Wattenberg's view that the current realignment, such as it is, is "hollow" because the parties have lost so much of their affective and cognitive centrality to citizens' mental maps of politics. If this is true, then the unquestioned rise in popular identification with the Republican party need not have the widespread political impact characteristic of previous partisan realignments. It simply reiterates what we already know, namely, that the Republican party has fielded more popular presidential candidates in recent years. And if so, the popular swing to the Republican party will last only as long as Republican administrations and presidential candidates maintain their popularity.

THE SOUTHERN STRATEGY REVISITED

The movement of voters into the Republican party has been most pronounced in the South, and so has Republican success in presidential elections. Since 1968, with but a single exception, only a Southerner— Jimmy Carter—has drawn any Southern state in the Democratic column.[7] In presidential elections, the Republicans' "Southern strategy" has proven remarkably effective.

The Southern strategy has been rather less effective in congressional elections. Partisan competition spread to Southern states during the late 1950s and early 1960s, but Southern House seats remain disproportionately in Democratic hands. More importantly, while Republicans were gaining seats in the South, Democrats were gaining even more seats elsewhere. These trends are documented in Figures 6.2 and 6.3.

Figure 6.2 traces the percentage of House seats won by Democratic candidates in the South and elsewhere from 1946 through 1988. Two things are noteworthy in these data. First, of course, is that as Republicans have won more seats in the South, Democrats have increased their share elsewhere. This trend coincides, not accidentally, with the growing number of unopposed Democrats and the declining quality of Republican challengers outside the South (documented in figures 4.5 and 4.7). Second, since the late 1960s, trends in the South have paralleled those in the rest of the country; national swings are no longer distinguishable by region. The change is, in statistical terms, striking: Between 1946 and 1964, interelection vote swings within the South were unrelated to those elsewhere ($r = .05$); since 1966, swings have been highly correlated across regions ($r = .82$). In aggregate, the South now moves with the rest of the country.

The regression slopes for the two trends displayed in Figure 6.2 are -1.85 and 1.13, respectively. In percentage terms, the Republicans gained more in the South than they lost elsewhere. But remember that the South holds only about one-quarter of all House seats. In actual seats,

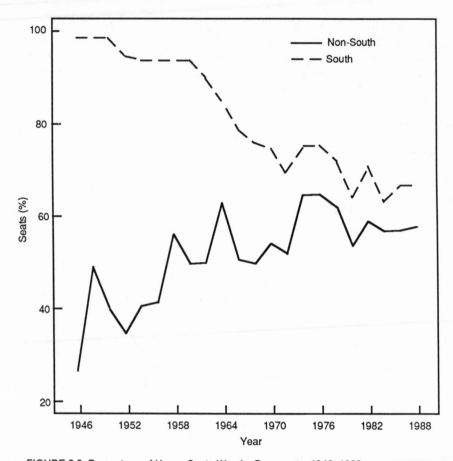

FIGURE 6.2 Percentage of House Seats Won by Democrats, 1946–1988

Republicans suffered a net loss from these changes. Figure 6.3 shows the trends in the total number of House seats held by Democrats within and outside the South. The regression slopes estimated for these trends are −1.62 and 3.45, suggesting that, on average, Democrats gained twice as many House seats as they lost from whatever political changes broke up the solid South and shrunk regional differences. The Republicans' Southern strategy may have been very effective in presidential politics, but it has been a net loser at the congressional level.

THRIVING ON DISUNITY

The comparative failure of the Republicans' "Southern strategy" at the congressional level points to a final explanation of why presidential

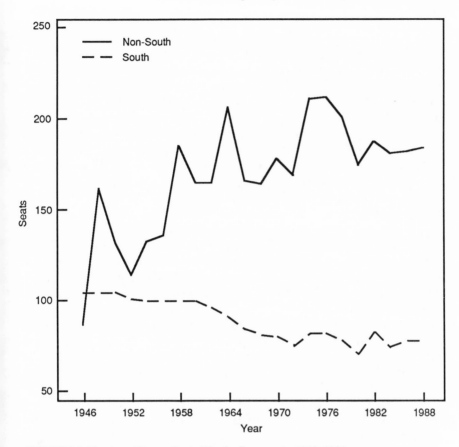

FIGURE 6.3 Number of House Seats Won by Democrats, 1946–1988

Republicans do so much better than congressional Republicans. This book has examined the electoral roots of divided government from the perspective of Republican difficulties in winning congressional elections. An alternative approach—requiring a rather different book—might just as well focus on Democratic difficulties in winning presidential elections. Their problems have already been documented (Chapter 1). In eleven postwar elections, Democratic presidential candidates have only once (in 1964) taken more than 50.1% of the total votes cast; Republicans have done so six times. Democratic presidential candidates in recent years have suffered from the perception that their party is subservient to a host of unfashionable "special interests," including organized labor, racial minorities, feminists, teachers, homosexuals, and other liberal activists (Miller, Hildreth, and Wlezien 1988). They have also suffered from the taint of "liberalism," portrayed as an inclination to tax and spend, excessive tolerance of social deviance, and a doubtful commitment to law and order at home and to American interests abroad.

Moreover, Democratic presidential candidates face a daunting task in trying to build a national coalition out of mutually antagonistic groups: blacks, Jews, working-class whites, Southern traditionalists, and affluent college-educated liberals. And they are handicapped in this endeavor by a nominating process that rewards candidates who can mobilize factions at the expense of those who attempt to build coalitions (Polsby 1983).

Congressional Democrats may do better simply because they do not face these problems. They are free to assemble local coalitions that may or may not include groups important to the party nationally. They can run as staunch friends of organized labor, civil rights activists, feminists, or the environmental movement when this adds votes, and they can avoid such alliances when it does not. A wide range of ideological stances is available to them; Southern Democrats, for example, can present themselves credibly as military hawks regardless of their party's national image. The fragmented, decentralized electoral process allows congressional Democrats to turn a severe national problem—diversity and discord—to local advantage. Moreover, they suffer little damage from the charge that Democrats are too solicitous of special interests because members of Congress are *expected* to serve special interests— those of their constituents. The same image that hurts presidential Democrats may, in this way, actually help congressional Democrats.

Conversely, the benefit Republican presidential candidates derive from perceptions that their party is better at promoting economic efficiency and growth, as well as other comprehensive collective goods, may not extend to Republican congressional candidates at all, especially if they can be portrayed as more interested in national issues than in local needs. In general, we would expect Republican Senate candidates to profit more from their party's reputation in this regard than Republican House candidates, if only because states are usually more populous and diverse than congressional districts and so encompass broader interests. This may be one reason Republicans have been so much more competitive in Senate contests during the Reagan-Bush years. Even so, Republican senators first elected on the Reagan ticket in 1980 who seemed more interested in pushing a national ideological agenda than in looking out for the home folks—notably Jeremiah Denton of Alabama and Mack Mattingly of Georgia—were defeated in 1986. Others who, like Alphonse D'Amato of New York and Charles Grassley of Iowa, worked diligently to serve state interests, won easy reelection.

In sum, Democratic weaknesses in presidential elections emerge as strengths in congressional elections. An ungainly national coalition lends itself to a wide diversity of state and district coalitions. Poor ideological focus hurts nationally but liberates locally. A reputation for sensitivity to "special interests" hobbles presidential Democrats; a reputation for sensitivity to local interests is bread and butter to congressional Democrats. Being thought of as the party of the welfare state has its disadvantages, but it seems to help in attracting talented people to careers in electoral politics.

AN OSSIFIED CONGRESS?

The record high reelection rate of House incumbents during the 1984–1988 election triad, perpetuating the Democrats' seemingly unassailable majority, has been portrayed by some observers as a failure of democracy. The overwhelming advantages of incumbency, financial and otherwise, deprive voters of a meaningful choice; the dearth of closely fought contests makes voting pointless in a large majority of districts. The low turnover of seats in 1988, according to the president of Common Cause, Fred Wertheimer, "simply reflects the fact that we don't have elections in the House of Representatives any more" (Rovner 1988:3362). Moreover, "if you don't have real elections, you don't have accountability. Democracy starts with elections, and if you have a rigged system, you don't have a representative government" (Rovner 1988:3365). Thus changes in public preferences expressed in presidential voting and in polling on party identification are echoed only faintly, if at all, in congressional elections. Divided party control of the federal government is an artifact of a structure that prevents Republicans from winning their rightful share of congressional seats.

The evidence I have presented in this book points to a rather different conclusion. The roots of divided government are political, not structural. The Democrats' continuing control of Congress expresses, rather than thwarts, the popular will. Electoral swings have been modest in recent elections because national conditions and issues have not been conducive to change. Anticipating little help from the political climate, both parties mounted relatively few strong challenges. It is scarcely surprising that inexperienced challengers lacking adequate funds and resonant issues should fail to defeat incumbents.

Obviously, it would be a mistake to infer from recent House elections that incumbents have become immune to national tides if no national tides were running. We only learn the true measure of an incumbent's strength when it is tested under adverse conditions by a vigorous challenge. The end-of-competition view is remarkably myopic; adequately financed challengers wielding potent issues swept a total of forty-nine incumbents out of office in 1980 and 1982. There is no reason to believe that such swings would not happen again under similar conditions. Indeed, the example of 1980 shows how fragile political support may be even for ostensibly entrenched incumbents in an era of fickle electorates.

There is, however, good reason for believing that the effect of both national and local issues is less automatic, more contingent, than it was in earlier decades. The increasingly fragmented, candidate-centered electoral politics that have emerged since 1946 have not made issues irrelevant, nor have they insulated incumbent members of Congress from national tides. They have, however, left the impact of issues more dependent on what the candidates do with them. Incumbents clearly find it easier now to escape the consequences of bad times or other threatening circumstances if they can manage to avoid challengers with the skills and resources to tag them with a share of the blame and to present an acceptable alternative. Voters are less willing to throw out rascals without knowing something about the rascals they would, at the same time, be throwing in. This means that unless its strategic politicians anticipate emerging opportunities and act accordingly, the party favored by national conditions will not benefit as much as it would have earlier; the premature concentration of resources discussed in Chapter 4 can thus mute the aggregate impact of national forces. It also means that a party suffering a shortage of attractive challengers will derive smaller benefit from favorable trends, a circumstance that has reinforced Republicans' difficulties in House elections.

THE FUTURE OF DIVIDED GOVERNMENT

What, then, are the prospects for electoral change? First, they are governed not by structure, but by politics. And the politics of divided government at present do not promise much change in the near future. Democratic congresses and Republican presidencies reinforce one another. Voters need not consciously divide control of government between the two parties for divided control to influence their voting decisions. Democratic majorities in Congress make a Republican presidential candidate's promise of "no new taxes" more appealing; at the same time, people may feel more comfortable voting for a Republican president knowing that the Democrats in Congress will keep him from gutting their favorite programs or invading Nicaragua. Conversely, it becomes more difficult to persuade voters to boot Democrats out of Congress when there is a Republican in the White House to control their collective excesses.

Credit for good times is shared, so incumbent Democrats are not threatened by successful Republican administrations. Indeed, the only serious threat to congressional Democrats in the past four decades has

TABLE 6.14
Presidential Politics and House Elections, 1946–1988

Presidential Politics	Democratic House Seats (Mean)
Democrats retain presidency (1948, 1964)	279
Democrats win presidency from Republicans (1960, 1976)	276
Republican president, midterm election (1954, 1958, 1970, 1974, 1982, 1986)	264
Republicans retain presidency (1956, 1972, 1984, 1988)	243
Democratic president, midterm election (1946, 1950, 1962, 1966, 1978)	241
Republicans win presidency from Democrats (1952, 1968, 1980)	233

come from failed Democratic administrations. The data in Table 6.14 show that Democrats have won fewest House seats when losing the presidency, second fewest at midterm elections with a Democrat in the White House. They have been slightly more successful when a Republican retains the presidency than at midterms under Democratic presidents. Only winning the presidency is more helpful to Democratic House candidates than midterms under Republican presidents. There is more than a grain of truth behind Robert Erikson's (1989) delightfully ironic demonstration that losing the presidency is a rational strategy for congressional Democrats.

Considering these patterns, the most plausible scenario for ending divided government is for a Democrat to win the presidency. All it would take is for a Republican administration to stumble badly and for the Democrats to nominate an acceptable alternative; neither is guaranteed, but neither is unimaginable, either. A Democratic presidency is also the only scenario offering Republicans much hope of making substantial gains, let alone winning majorities, in Congress during the remainder of the century.

For the foreseeable future, however, the current partisan division of government is likely to continue. As of this writing (March 1990), the 1990 elections promise little change: No strong national forces are evident; the economy is growing, albeit slowly, and unemployment remains low; and the recession that has been anticipated so often since the last one in 1982 is still no more than a rumor. Scandals have not taken a form that would lend itself to partisan use, and the most vulnerable individual incumbents have already resigned. The usual midterm swing against the president's party is not likely to be very large, if only because Democrats already hold so many seats. Thus another quiet election, with few seats changing party control, is likely.

Prospects for 1992 are less certain, and by no means only because it lies farther in the future. The House will be reapportioned and its districts redrawn after 1990. Not only will this shuffle the deck, but the prospect of a new deal should embolden potential challengers and contributors to take the steps that are necessary, if not sufficient, to produce major electoral changes. Leaders of both parties are already looking beyond 1990 to 1992, Republicans with renewed hope, Democrats with considerable trepidation. The coincidence of new district lines, parity in party identification, and a Republican president running for reelection appear to brighten Republican chances of making serious progress in the House. But if my interpretation of postwar electoral history is on target, it will take a good deal more than this conjunction of events to produce a unified Republican federal government.

Does this mean an end to representative government? Has democratic responsiveness disappeared? Of course not. There is something perverse about the argument that a system in which legislators enjoy high rates of reelection must be less representative of citizens' preferences than one in which wholesale replacement of incumbents is the norm. Members of Congress get reelected by doing what people want them to do; the perfectly responsive representative would presumably never lose. The problem is that individual responsiveness undermines collective responsibility (Fiorina 1980; Jacobson 1987b). Of course, whatever undermines collective responsibility in a Democratic Congress simply reinforces voters' incentives to elect Republican presidents.

NOTES

1. One item of evidence in the thesis's favor: Burnham (1985) reports a September 1984 Yankelovich Poll in which 4% of the respondents intending to vote for Reagan said that this would make it *less* likely that they would vote for Republicans for other offices (29% replied more likely, 65% said it would make no difference).

2. All of the questions and results in Tables 6.1 through 6.9 are from the *New York Times*/CBS News Poll National Surveys (except for part of question 1 in Table 6.3, which is taken from the 1986 American National Election Study). The polls were conducted by telephone; the typical sample includes about 1,500 respondents. Individual surveys are identified by date; in months with more than one survey, the first is designated "A," the second, "B," and so forth. For all questions, responses "both," "both equal," "neither," and "depends" were not given as options in the question but were volunteered by the respondent.

3. Except under very restricted—and politically rare—circumstances (Olson 1965; Hardin 1982).

4. Mark Zupan's (1989) discovery that House Republicans have somewhat smaller personal staffs (an average of 13.9 persons, compared to 14.5 for Democrats) and put fewer of them in the district (41.3%, compared to 46.6%) also stands as circumstantial evidence for the notion that Republicans engage in less assiduous cultivation of their districts, although Zupan's data necessarily tell an ambiguous story because they are drawn from only those Republicans who have chosen to enter and remain in the House and so pay as much attention to the district as they think they must.

5. The cumulative results of seven *New York Times*/CBS News Polls conducted during 1989 (N = 8,719) found 46% of the respondents calling themselves Democrats, 44%, Republicans (*San Diego Union*, January 21, 1990, p. A-10).

6. Michael MacKuen, personal communication, November 16, 1989.

7. The exception is Hubert Humphrey's 1968 victory in Texas, which was probably more Lyndon Johnson's than Humphrey's doing.

References

Abramowitz, Alan I. 1983. Partisan Redistricting and the 1982 Congressional Elections. *Journal of Politics* 45:767–770.

Alesina, Alberto, and Howard Rosenthal. 1989. Partisan Cycles in Congressional Elections and the Macroeconomy. *American Political Science Review* 83:373–398.

Alford, John, and David W. Brady. 1988. Partisan and Incumbent Advantage in U.S. House Elections, 1846–1986. Working Paper Number 11. Center for the Study of Institutions and Values, Rice University.

Alston, Chuck, and Glen Craney. 1989. Bush Campaign-Reform Plan Takes Aim at Incumbents. *Congressional Quarterly Weekly Report* (July 1):1648–1659.

Ansolabehere, Stephen, David W. Brady, and Morris P. Fiorina. 1988. The Marginals Never Vanished? Working Papers in Political Science P-88-1. The Hoover Institution, Stanford University.

Arcelus, Francisco, and Allan H. Meltzer. 1975. The Effects of Aggregate Economic Variables on Congressional Elections. *American Political Science Review* 69:232–239.

Barone, Michael, and Grant Ujifusa. 1987. *The Almanac of American Politics 1988.* Washington, D.C.: National Journal.

————. 1989. *The Almanac of American Politics 1990.* Washington, D.C.: National Journal.

Bauer, Monica, and John R. Hibbing. 1989. Which Incumbents Lose in House Elections: A Reply to Jacobson's The Marginals Never Vanished. *American Journal of Political Science* 33:262–271.

Bianco, William T. 1984. Strategic Decisions on Candidacy in U.S. Congressional Districts. *Legislative Studies Quarterly* 9:351–364. Washington, D.C.: U.S. Government Printing Office.

Biographical Directory of the American Congress, 1774–1971. 1971. Washington, D.C.: U.S. Government Printing Office.

Bloom, Howard S., and H. Douglas Price. 1975. Voter Response to Short-Run Economic Conditions: The Asymmetric Effect of Prosperity and Recession. *American Political Science Review* 69:1240–1254.

Bond, Jon R., Cary Covington, and Richard Fleisher. 1985. Explaining Challenger Quality in Congressional Elections. *Journal of Politics* 47:510–529.

Born, Richard. 1984. Reassessing the Decline of Presidential Coattails: U.S. House Elections from 1952–80. *Journal of Politics* 46:60–79.

―――. 1985. Partisan Intentions and Election Day Realities in the Congressional Redistricting Process. *American Political Science Review* 79:304–319.

―――. 1986. Strategic Politicians and Unresponsive Voters. *American Political Science Review* 80:599–612.

Burnham, Walter Dean. 1975. Insulation and Responsiveness in Congressional Elections. *Political Science Quarterly* 90:411–435.

―――. 1985. The 1984 Election and the Future of American Politics. In *Election '84: Landslide Without a Mandate?* ed. Ellis Sandoz and Cecil V. Crabb, Jr. New York: New American Library.

Cain, Bruce E. 1984. *The Reapportionment Puzzle.* Berkeley and Los Angeles: University of California Press.

Cain, Bruce E., and Janet C. Campagna. 1987. Predicting Partisan Redistricting Disputes. *Legislative Studies Quarterly* 12:265–274.

Calvert, Randall L., and John A. Ferejohn. 1983. Coattail Voting in Recent Presidential Elections. *American Political Science Review* 77:407–419.

Campbell, Angus. 1960. Surge and Decline: A Study of Electoral Change. *Public Opinion Quarterly* 24:397–418.

Campbell, James E. 1986. Predicting Seat Gains from Presidential Coattails. *American Journal of Political Science* 30:165–183.

Canon, David T. 1985. Political Conditions and Experienced Challengers in Congressional Elections, 1972–1984. Paper delivered at the Annual Meeting of the American Political Science Association, New Orleans, Louisiana, August 29–September 1, 1985.

Cloud, David S. 1988. Feud Between GOP, PACs Stings Candidates. *Congressional Quarterly Weekly Report* (September 3):2447–2450.

Common Cause. 1974. *1972 Congressional Campaign Finances,* 10 vols. Washington, D.C.: Common Cause.

―――. 1976. *1974 Congressional Campaign Finances,* 3 vols. Washington, D.C.: Common Cause.

Congressional Quarterly. 1985. *Guide to U.S. Elections,* 2d ed. Washington, D.C.: Congressional Quarterly.

―――. Various issues. *Congressional Quarterly Weekly Report.* Washington, D.C.: Congressional Quarterly.

Cook, Rhodes. 1989. Is Competition in Elections Becoming Obsolete? *Congressional Quarterly Weekly Report* (May 6):1060–1065.

Cover, Albert D. 1977. One Good Term Deserves Another: The Advantage of Incumbency in Congressional Elections. *American Journal of Political Science* 24:523–542.

Cover, Albert D., and David R. Mayhew. 1981. Congressional Dynamics and the Decline of Competitive Congressional Elections. In *Congress Reconsidered,* 2d ed., ed. Lawrence C. Dodd and Bruce I. Oppenheimer. Washington, D.C.: Congressional Quarterly Press.

Edwards, George C., III. 1980. *Presidential Influence in Congress.* San Francisco: W. H. Freeman.

Election Index. 1966, 1968, 1970, 1972, 1974, 1976, 1978, 1980, 1982. Mt. Vernon, Virginia: Congressional Staff Directory.

Erikson, Robert S. 1972. Malapportionment, Gerrymandering, and Party Fortunes in Congressional Elections. *American Political Science Review* 66:1234–1245.

———. 1989. Why the Democrats Lose Presidential Elections. *PS: Political Science & Politics* 22:30–34.

———. 1990a. Economic Conditions and the Congressional Vote: A Review of the Macrolevel Evidence. *American Journal of Political Science*, in press.

———. 1990b. Reply to Jacobson. *American Journal of Political Science*, in press.

Federal Election Commission. 1977. *Disclosure Series No. 9* (House of Representatives Campaigns). Washington, D.C.: Federal Election Commission.

———. 1979. *FEC Reports on Financial Activity, 1977–1978, Interim Report No. 5: U.S. Senate and House Campaigns.* Washington, D.C.: Federal Election Commission.

———. 1982. *FEC Reports on Financial Activity, 1979–1980, Final Report: U.S. Senate and House Campaigns.* Washington, D.C.: Federal Election Commission.

———. 1983. *FEC Reports on Financial Activity, 1981–1982, Interim Report No. 3: U.S. Senate and House Campaigns.* Washington, D.C.: Federal Election Commission.

———. 1985. *FEC Reports on Financial Activity, 1983–1984, Interim Report No. 9: U.S. Senate and House Campaigns.* Washington, D.C.: Federal Election Commission.

Fenno, Richard F., Jr. 1978. *Home Style: House Members in Their Districts.* Boston: Little, Brown.

Ferejohn, John A. 1977. On the Decline of Competition in Congressional Elections. *American Political Science Review* 71:166–176.

Ferejohn, John A., and Randall L. Calvert. 1984. Presidential Coattails in Historical Perspective. *American Journal of Political Science* 28:127–146.

Fiorina, Morris P. 1980. The Decline of Collective Responsibility in American Politics. *Daedalus* 109:25–45.

———. 1981a. *Retrospective Voting in American National Elections.* New Haven, Connecticut: Yale University Press.

———. 1981b. Some Problems in Studying the Effects of Resource Allocation in Congressional Elections. *American Journal of Political Science* 25:543–567.

———. 1988. The Reagan Years: Turning to the Right or Groping Toward the Middle? In *The Resurgence of Conservatism in Anglo-American Democracies*, ed. Barry Cooper, Allan Kornberg, and William Mishler. Durham, North Carolina: Duke University Press.

———. 1989. *Congress: Keystone of the Washington Establishment*, 2d ed. New Haven, Connecticut: Yale University Press.

———. 1990. An Era of Divided Government. In *Developments in American Politics*, ed. Bruce Cain and Gillian Peele. London: Macmillan.

Fiorina, Morris P., and Douglas Rivers. 1989. Constituency Service, Reputation, and the Incumbency Advantage. In *Home Style and Congressional Work*, ed. Morris P. Fiorina and David Rohde. Ann Arbor: University of Michigan Press.

Gelman, Andrew, and Gary King. 1989. Estimating the Incumbency Advantage Without Bias. Unpublished paper.

Green, Donald P. October 1989. Personal communication.

142   *References*

Gudgin, Graham, and Peter Taylor. 1979. *Seats, Votes, and the Spatial Organization of Elections.* London: Pion Press.
Hardin, Russell. 1982. *Collective Action.* Baltimore, Maryland: Johns Hopkins University Press.
Herrnson, Paul S. 1988. *Party Campaigning in the 1980s.* Cambridge, Massachusetts: Harvard University Press.
Hibbing, John R. 1982. Voluntary Retirements from the House in the Twentieth Century. *Journal of Politics* 44:1020–1034.
Hook, Janet. 1988. House's 1980 "Reagan Robots" Face Crossroads. *Congressional Quarterly Weekly Report* (August 13):2262–2265.
Iyengar, Shanto, and Donald R. Kinder. 1987. *News that Matters: Television and American Opinion.* Chicago: University of Chicago Press.
Jackson, Brooks. 1988. *Honest Graft: Big Money and the American Political Process.* New York: Alfred A. Knopf.
Jacobson, Gary C. 1980. *Money in Congressional Elections.* New Haven, Connecticut: Yale University Press.
———. 1985a. Congress: Politics After a Landslide Without Coattails. In *The Elections of 1984,* ed. Michael Nelson. Washington, D.C.: Congressional Quarterly.
———. 1985b. Money and Votes Reconsidered: Congressional Elections, 1972–1982. *Public Choice* 47:7–62.
———. 1985–1986. Party Organization and Distribution of Campaign Resources: Republicans and Democrats in 1982. *Political Science Quarterly* 100:603–625.
———. 1987a. The Marginals Never Vanished: Incumbency and Competition in Elections to the U.S. House of Representatives. *American Journal of Political Science* 31:126–141.
———. 1987b. *The Politics of Congressional Elections.* Boston: Little, Brown.
———. 1987c. Enough Is Too Much: Money and Competition in House Elections, 1972–1984. In *Elections in America,* ed. Kay L. Schlozman. New York: Allen and Unwin.
———. 1988. Parties and PACs in Congressional Elections. In *Congress Reconsidered,* ed. Lawrence C. Dodd and Bruce I. Oppenheimer. Washington, D.C.: Congressional Quarterly Press.
———. 1989. Strategic Politicians and the Dynamics of U.S. House Elections, 1946–1986. *American Political Science Review* 83:773–793.
———. 1990a. Does the Economy Matter in Midterm Elections? *American Journal of Political Science* 34:400–404.
———. 1990b. The Effects of Campaign Spending in House Elections: New Evidence for Old Arguments. *American Journal of Political Science* 34:334–362.
———. 1990c. Meager Patrimony: Republican Representation in Congress After Reagan. In *The Reagan Imprint,* ed. Larry Berman. Baltimore, Maryland: Johns Hopkins University Press.
Jacobson, Gary C., and Samuel Kernell. 1983. *Strategy and Choice in Congressional Elections,* 2d ed. New Haven, Connecticut: Yale University Press.
———. 1990. National Forces in the 1986 House Elections. *Legislative Studies Quarterly* 15:65–87.

Johannes, John R., and John C. McAdams. 1981. The Congressional Incumbency Effect: Is It Casework, Policy Compatibility, or Something Else? *American Journal of Political Science* 25:512–542.

Jones, Charles O. 1981. New Directions in U.S. Congressional Research. *Legislative Studies Quarterly* 6:458.

Keith, Bruce E., David B. Magleby, Candice J. Nelson, Elizabeth Orr, Mark Westlye, and Raymond E. Wolfinger. 1977. The Myth of the Independent Voter. Paper delivered at the Annual Meeting of the American Political Science Association, Washington, D.C., September 1–4, 1977.

Kiewiet, D. Roderick, and Douglas Rivers. 1985. The Economic Basis of Reagan's Appeal. In *The New Direction in American Politics*, ed. John E. Chubb and Paul E. Peterson. Washington, D.C.: Brookings Institution.

King, Gary, and Robert X. Browning. 1987. Democratic Representation and Partisan Bias in Congressional Elections. *American Political Science Review* 81:1251–1273.

King, Gary, and Andrew Gelman. 1988. Systemic Consequences of Incumbency Advantage in U.S. House Elections. Unpublished paper, Harvard University.

King, Gary, and Lyn Ragsdale. 1988. *The Elusive Executive*. Washington, D.C.: Congressional Quarterly Press.

Kramer, Gerald H. 1971. Short-Term Fluctuations in U.S. Voting Behavior, 1896–1964. *American Political Science Review* 65:131–143.

Krasno, Jonathan S., and Donald Philip Green. 1988. Preempting Quality Challengers in House Elections. *Journal of Politics* 50:920–936.

MacKuen, Michael B., Robert S. Erikson, and James A. Stimson. 1989. Macropartisanship. *American Political Science Review* 83:1125–1142.

Maisel, Louis Sandy. 1982. *From Obscurity to Oblivion: Running in the Congressional Primaries*. Knoxville: University of Tennessee Press.

Mayhew, David R. 1974a. *Congress: The Electoral Connection*. New Haven, Connecticut: Yale University Press.

———. 1974b. Congressional Elections: The Case of the Vanishing Marginals. *Polity* 6:295–317.

Miller, Arthur H., Ann Hildreth, and Christopher Wlezien. 1988. Social Group Dynamics of Political Evaluations. Paper delivered at the Annual Meeting of the Midwest Political Science Association, Chicago, Illinois, April 14–16, 1988.

Mondak, Jeffrey J. 1989. Could George Bush Have Had Coattails?: Republican Opportunities in 1988. Paper delivered at the Annual Meeting of the American Political Science Association, Atlanta, Georgia, August 31–September 3, 1989.

Niemi, Richard G., and Patrick Fett. 1986. The Swing Ratio: An Explanation and Assessment. *Legislative Studies Quarterly* 11:75–90.

Olson, Mancur. 1965. *The Logic of Collective Action: Public Goods and the Theory of Groups*. Cambridge, Massachusetts: Harvard University Press.

Oppenheimer, Bruce I., James A. Stimson, and Richard W. Waterman. 1986. Interpreting U.S. Congressional Elections: The Exposure Thesis. *Legislative Studies Quarterly* 11:227–247.

Ornstein, Norman J., Thomas E. Mann, and Michael Malbin. 1990. *Vital Statistics on Congress 1989–1990*. Washington, D.C.: Congressional Quarterly Press.

Polsby, Nelson W. 1983. *The Consequences of Party Reform*. Oxford: Oxford University Press.

Popkin, Samuel, J. W. Gorman, C. Phillips, and J. A. Smith. 1976. Comment: What Have You Done for Me Lately? Toward an Investment Theory of Voting. *American Political Science Review* 70:779–805.

Robertson, Andrew W. 1983. American Redistricting in the 1980s: The Effect on the Midterm Elections. *Electoral Studies* 2:113–129.

Rovner, Julie. 1988. Turnover in Congress Hits an All-Time Low. *Congressional Quarterly Weekly Report* (November 19):3362–3365.

Tufte, Edward R. 1973. The Relationship Between Seats and Votes in Two-Party Systems. *American Political Science Review* 67:540–547.

_____ . 1975. Determinants of the Outcomes of Midterm Congressional Elections. *American Political Science Review* 69:816–826.

_____ . 1978. *Political Control of the Economy*. Princeton, New Jersey: Princeton University Press.

U.S. Council of Economic Advisors. 1987. *Economic Report of the President*. Washington, D.C.: U.S. Government Printing Office.

_____ . 1989. *Economic Report of the President*. Washington, D.C.: U.S. Government Printing Office.

U.S. Department of Commerce, Bureau of Economic Analysis. 1981. *The National Income and Product Accounts of the United States, 1929–76, Statistical Tables*. Washington, D.C.: U.S. Government Printing Office.

_____ . Various issues. *Survey of Current Business*. Washington, D.C.: U.S. Government Printing Office.

Wattenberg, Martin P. 1990. *The Decline of American Political Parties: 1952–1988*. Cambridge, Massachusetts: Harvard University Press.

Wilcox, Clyde. 1987. The Timing of Strategic Decisions: Candidacy Decisions in 1982 and 1984. *Legislative Studies Quarterly* 12:565–572.

Wilcox, Clyde, and Bob Biersack. 1990. Research Update: The Timing of Candidacy Decisions in the House, 1982–1988. *Legislative Studies Quarterly* 15:115–126.

Zupan, Mark A. 1989. An Economic Explanation for the Existence and Nature of Political Ticket Splitting. Unpublished paper, University of Southern California School of Business.

About the Book and Author

Is divided government—a Republican president and a Democratic Congress—the product of diminished competition for seats in the U.S. House of Representatives? In this groundbreaking study, Gary C. Jacobson uses a detailed analysis of the evolution of competition in postwar House elections to argue that the problems Republicans face in seeking House seats are political rather than structural.

With abundant graphic illustration, he shows that divided government is only one piece of a much broader electoral pattern that is creating new opportunities as well as new barriers to partisan change in the House. He examines shifts in the incumbency advantage, campaign finance practices, the "swing ratio," and other related phenomena, but he turns up little evidence that they are to blame for divided government.

More important, he argues, are trends in partisan opposition: the quality of candidates, campaigns, issues, and career strategies. As individual candidates and campaigns have become more important in winning elections, the weakness of Republican House candidacies has prevented the party from taking more seats away from the Democrats.

Jacobson contends that the House is not nearly as insulated from electoral change as recent elections might suggest. The notion that House elections are no longer capable of reflecting popular preferences is, he concludes, simply wrong.

Gary C. Jacobson is professor of political science at the University of California–San Diego and author of numerous articles and several books, including *The Politics of Congressional Elections, Strategy and Choice in Congressional Elections* (with Samuel Kernell), and *Money in Congressional Elections*, which won the 1980 Gladys M. Kammerer Award for the best publication in the field of U.S. national policy.

Index

American National Election Studies, 9, 126, 128

Baker v. *Carr*, 94
Budget issues, 106–109, 111, 115, 119
  public opinion on, 107(table), 108(table), 109(table)
Bush, George, 1, 45, 65, 125
  on gerrymandering, 94
  influence of, 14–15

Campaign finance system, 3, 75, 96–102
  See also Resources; Campaign spending
Campaign spending, 73(n5), 97(fig.), 99(fig.), 101(table)
  concentration of, 69, 70(fig.), 71(fig.)
  decline of, 63, 65, 106, 122
  experienced candidates and, 54, 123
  marginal returns on, 54–55, 100
  for open seats, 64(fig.), 98(fig.)
  reactive, 55, 101
  See also Campaign finance system; Resources
Candidate-centered electoral politics, 55, 92
  growth of, 2, 3, 21, 23(n10), 32, 50, 134
Candidates, Democratic
  national tides and, 92
  PAC contributions to, 100(fig.)

problems for, 120–121, 131–133
  quality of, 62(fig.), 74(n11)
  spending by, 64(fig.), 71(fig.), 98(fig.), 99(fig.), 100–101
  spending for, 102
  See also Candidates, experienced; Candidates, inexperienced; Candidates, Republican
Candidates, experienced, 42, 45–46, 52, 59(table), 82, 136
  avoiding, 134
  fielding, 50–51, 58, 60, 67, 105, 115
  ideology and, 120–122
  importance of, 15, 61, 65–66, 72
  open seats and, 66(table), 68(fig.), 68(table)
  partisan differences in, 67
  percentage of, 61(table)
  probability of victory of, 52–53
  quality of, 56(table), 59(fig.)
  shortage of, 134
  spending by, 101(table)
  spending on, 102, 123
  vote shift and, 41(table)
  See also Candidates, Democratic; Candidates, inexperienced; Candidates, Republican; Experience; Quality of House candidates
Candidates, inexperienced, 48, 54, 65, 92, 123, 133
  impact of, 55–57
  incumbency advantage and, 57–58
  national conditions and, 42, 58, 60

147

Expectations, electoral
  effect of, 52
  voter, 106, 112–120
Expenditure, variables determining,
  54. *See also* Campaign spending
Experience
  decline in, 65
  importance of, 50–54, 102
  measurement of, 72–73(n3)
  victory frequency and, 51(table),
    53(table)
  See also Candidates, experienced;
    Quality of House candidates

Federal Election Campaign Act of
  1973, 96
Ford, Gerald, 79
Franking privilege, abuse of, 1
Freshmen
  defeat of, 121
  reelection of, 19–20
  See also Candidates, experienced;
    Candidates, inexperienced
Fund raising, 1, 54

Gerrymandering, 1, 3, 15, 75, 102
  impact of, 94–96
  See also Redistricting
Gingrich, Newt, quote of, 1
Goldwater, Barry, impact of, 46
Grassley, Charles, reelection of, 132
Growth, collective goods and, 111

Hiler, John, 121
  quote of, 120
House seats
  Democratic, 8(fig.)
  marginal, 29(table)
  predicted by regression models,
    88(table)
  presidency and, 6(fig.), 135(table)
  Southern, 130(fig.), 131(fig.)
  state elections and, 14(table), 76,
    78(fig.), 78(table)
  switching party control, 91(table)

Incumbency advantage, 3, 14, 15, 20,
  23(n10), 31(fig.), 43(n5), 37–38,
  87, 102, 133
  articles on, 25
  challengers and, 57–58
  exaggeration of, 21–22
  growth of, 63
  mean vote percentage and, 29
  measuring, 26–32
  national swings and, 82
  partisan component of, 32, 93–94
  redistricting and, 94–95
  spending and, 69, 71–72
  value of, 2, 12, 16, 17, 19, 29–30,
    32, 45, 72
Incumbents
  defeat of, 30, 32, 33, 40, 42
  marginal, 26, 28(fig.), 28–29
  national tides and, 19, 41(table),
    89, 92, 133
  spending by, 55, 64(fig.), 65, 96,
    101
  swing ratios and, 87, 89, 90
  success of, 38(fig.), 39(table)
  unopposed, 47(fig.), 48, 57
  vote shares and, 27(fig.), 39
  See also Incumbents, Democratic;
    Incumbents, Republican
Incumbents, Democratic
  national tides and, 92
  PACs and, 98–99, 100(fig.)
  Republican challengers and, 62–63
  threats to, 134–135
  spending by, 97(fig.)
  unopposed, 49(fig.), 50(fig.)
  See also Incumbents; Incumbents,
    Republican
Incumbents, Republican
  defeat of, 121
  national tides and, 92
  PACs and, 100(fig.)
  spending by, 97(fig.)
  unopposed, 49(fig.), 50(fig.)
  See also Incumbents; Incumbents,
    Democratic
Independents, turnout of, 9